HALF IN, HALF OUT

PRIME MINISTERS ON EUROPE

HALF IN HALF OUT

ANDREW ADONIS

Biteback Publishing

First published in Great Britain in 2018 by
Biteback Publishing Ltd
Westminster Tower
3 Albert Embankment
London SE1 7SP

ISBN 978-1-78590-434-9

10 9 8 7 6 5 4 3 2 1

A CIP catalogue record for this book is available from the British Library.

Set in Minion Pro

Printed and bound in Great Britain by
CPI Group (UK) Ltd, Croydon CR0 4YY

FSC
www.fsc.org
MIX
Paper from responsible sources
FSC® C020471

To the memory of Winston Churchill, who saved Europe and inspired the European Union.

'In the nightmare of the dark
All the dogs of Europe bark'

W. H. AUDEN

CONTENTS

THE AUTHORS

ANDREW ADONIS is author of *Saving Britain: How We Must Change to Prosper in Europe* (with Will Hutton) and a former minister under Tony Blair and Gordon Brown.

DAVID DUTTON is author of *Anthony Eden: A Life and Reputation* and Professor of Political History at Liverpool University.

DAVID FABER is headmaster of Summer Fields School, Oxford, a former Conservative MP and author of *Munich: The 1938 Appeasement Crisis.*

ANDREW HOLT is a historian of twentieth-century foreign policy and author of *The Foreign Policy of the Douglas-Home Government: Britain, the United States and the End of Empire.*

MICHAEL McMANUS is author of *Edward Heath: A Singular Life* and of *An Honourable Man*, a play asking the question 'What if the bitter wounds caused by Brexit do not heal?'

DAVID OWEN was Foreign Secretary under James Callaghan, 1977–79, Labour/SDP MP for Plymouth, 1966–92, and Leader of the SDP, 1983–87.

CHRIS PATTEN was a Cabinet minister under Margaret Thatcher, Conservative Party chairman and Governor of Hong Kong under John Major and Tony Blair, and is Chancellor of Oxford University.

CHARLES POWELL, Lord Powell of Bayswater, was foreign affairs private secretary to Margaret Thatcher and John Major, 1983–91.

RACHEL REEVES is MP for Leeds West and a former economist at the Bank of England and the British embassy in Washington.

STEVE RICHARDS presents Radio 4's *Week in Westminster* and is author of *Reflections on Leadership: Modern Prime Ministers from Heath to May*.

SIR IVAN ROGERS was Britain's Permanent Representative to the European Union, 2013–17, and principal private secretary to Tony Blair.

SIR NICHOLAS SOAMES is Conservative MP for Mid Sussex and was Minister for the Armed Forces under John Major.

STEWART WOOD, Lord Wood of Anfield, was adviser on Europe to Gordon Brown and fellow of Magdalen College, Oxford.

PREFACE

ANDREW ADONIS

The title *Half In, Half Out* aptly sums up the European policy of the British state since 'Victory in Europe' on 8 May 1945.

I thought, on an initial mental overview, that it also summed up the European policy of each of the fourteen Prime Ministers since 1945. Some were marginally more pro- or anti-European than others – but the degrees of difference were fairly small in terms of actual policy, which followed the broad centre-ground consensus at each stage.

All fourteen Prime Ministers sought, I thought, to reconcile *raison d'état* with *vox populi*, and the result was realpolitik.

Having engaged closely with each of the fourteen holders of the supreme office since 1945, in and through these essays, I have reached a radically different conclusion. I now suggest that they represent a wide spectrum of views on Europe within the British political class. At each stage, there was no consensus on future policy, except to the extent that the Prime Minister of the day was able to forge one. Far from being preordained, policy was highly contingent on each of their prejudices and preferences.

Only by according fundamental importance to the European policy of each individual Prime Minister since 1945, and grasping the differences between them, can one explain why we didn't go into Europe in the 1940s and 1950s (the intense Euroscepticism of Attlee and Eden, opposed by Churchill in opposition but not in office); why we tried to do so in the 1960s (Macmillan and Wilson led strongly in favour); why we succeeded in doing so in the 1970s (Heath led where Macmillan and Wilson had left off and Wilson, confronting a hostile party in office for a second time, manoeuvred successfully to keep Britain in); and then why we refused to integrate further in the decades after the 1990s, as Thatcher launched modern Euroscepticism and her successors Major, Blair, Brown and Cameron, sharing or fearing it to varying extents, sought largely to maintain the status quo except on the Social Chapter and enlargement of the EU to central and Eastern Europe. It also explains why David Cameron held an in/out referendum in 2016 (a leadership gamble that went catastrophically wrong), and why Theresa May is attempting 'hard Brexit' in 2018 (because she is intent on it, although she is not clear in her own mind or public statements quite what 'it' is).

At every point since 1945, European policy could have been different under different leadership. So today, and so in future.

Leadership matters. Ideas matter. They both matter fundamentally. Jonathan Freedland's profound insight into political behaviour – 'people don't believe in ideas, they believe in people who believe in ideas' – shines through this book leader by leader.

A second conclusion emanates. Until the 2016 referendum, not one of the fourteen Prime Ministers sought in office to disengage from Europe to any marked degree, whatever the state of European relations they inherited. Nor did they seriously wish to do so. In this respect, there was indeed a consensus based on a practical assessment of the realm of the possible, whether desirable or not; and this consensus held until the referendum on 23 June 2016.

Margaret Thatcher, the most dominant Prime Minister after Churchill in wartime, is highly ambiguous. Her European policy shifted dramatically at different stages of her premiership, as did Churchill's before and after taking office in 1951. In her first years, she was a tough, unsentimental negotiator within the EU, but not sceptical so far as membership itself was concerned. Mid-term she became a remarkable force for Euro integration in the creation of the single market. Then, in 1988, came her showdown on 'social Europe' with the socialist President of the Commission, Jacques Delors. This gave rise to her Bruges speech of 20 September 1988, perhaps the single most influential prime ministerial statement on Europe in the seventy-three years under review, akin to Churchill's Zurich speech of 1946, made when he was Leader of the Opposition. But even after 1988 – indeed within the Bruges speech itself – there was uncertainty and outright contradictions, reflecting Thatcher's characteristic ambiguity when departing from establishment views and veering sharply right.

It is time for bold, credible leadership on Europe. 'Where there is no vision the people perish.' As a strong pro-European, I see putting bold leadership back into the EU as imperative, and

I draw inspiration from the two remarkable essays here by grandsons on their grandfathers – Sir Nicholas Soames on Churchill and David Faber on Macmillan. But if we are to leave, we need to leave with a plan that works, and there is none at present.

Some of these essays began as the Hertford Lectures, which were generously hosted by Will Hutton, the principal of Hertford College, Oxford, and supported by Sir Clive Cowdery and *Prospect* magazine. Iain Dale, with his brilliant political and publishing insight, immediately said that the story had to go back to Churchill to make sense, and encouraged me to publish on the second anniversary of the 2016 referendum. I am hugely grateful to Charlie Atkins, Olivia Beattie, Max Wind-Cowie, Roger Liddle and Bernadette Marron for comments and assistance on the way to publication.

Not all those who led decisively for and against British engagement in the European Union were Prime Ministers. Nigel Farage shares responsibility for Brexit with Margaret Thatcher, David Cameron and Theresa May, while Roy Jenkins stands alongside Churchill, Macmillan, Heath and Wilson for taking us in.

Farage, who never held a responsible post of national leadership, is tellingly the only leader to break from the consensus on 'staying in once in'. All the others share the credit for keeping the show on the road, without crisis leading either to war or economic collapse. In the long view of history, maybe that's as good as it gets.

Andrew Adonis
Westminster, 1 June 2018

CHAPTER I

WINSTON CHURCHILL

NICHOLAS SOAMES AND ANDREW ADONIS*

When the Nazi power was broken, I asked myself what was the best advice I could give to my fellow citizens here in this island and across the channel in our ravaged continent. There was no difficulty in answering the question. My counsel to Europe can be given in a single word: Unite!

CHURCHILL, 1947

The 1945 election result was an intense disappointment to Winston Churchill. He won a House of Commons majority of only sixty seats, having expected a landslide after his valiant wartime leadership. But, after hearing the results on 26 July, he immediately returned to the Potsdam Conference with

* This essay was written by Andrew Adonis after conversations with Nicholas Soames.

Stalin and Truman in occupied Germany and turned his mind to reshaping the post-war world. What happened next is a remarkable story.

• • •

The experience of the Yalta Conference, which met to consider the future of central and Eastern Europe in February 1945, was searing. Churchill was forced to cede to Stalin suzerainty over half of Germany, much of the Balkans and all of Poland, Hungary and Czechoslovakia. This was partly because of Uncle Joe's ruthless ascendancy after defeating and occupying Germany from the East, but also partly because of the weakness of Roosevelt, ill and close to death, who thought he had a partnership with Stalin, and who distrusted British imperialism almost as much as Soviet communism. Churchill well knew that flimsy promises of multi-party elections in the territories relinquished to Stalin's overlordship amounted to, in effect, a sentence of domination and even annexation.

Churchill had a brilliant instinct for power: how to get it, how to wield it and how to recognise it in others. After Yalta, Potsdam and Truman's detonation of nuclear bombs over Hiroshima and Nagasaki in August 1945, Churchill saw in Stalin and Truman the arbiters of the globe. He saw too that Britain and Europe's interests lay unambiguously with the US. 'Not quite as wicked, but much more formidable than Hitler,' was his clear-sighted view of Stalin. He had none of the left's initial sentimental wishful thinking about 'Uncle Joe', which persisted not only in Continental communist and socialist parties, but even in much of Attlee's Labour Party, despite the systematic elimination of democracy across the Soviet Bloc after 1945.

Churchill's March 1946 Iron Curtain speech was the transformational moment, delivered in the presence of Truman in Fulton, Missouri. Controversial with the European left, and considered too anti-Russian by Truman at the time, it was soon regarded as prophetic by the US President and gave Churchill great sway thereafter as 'the man who got it right'.

The Fulton speech had two seminal effects. It gave an impetus to Churchill's plan to unite the Continent's Western democracies behind British leadership; and, as Truman came to share Churchill's analysis, it led the US to back the European union with a US defence commitment to its constituent members through what became NATO.

Hence the two dramatic developments of Churchill's 1945–49 government, both in 1948 and closely interrelated: the North Atlantic Treaty, which established NATO, and the Treaty of Paris, which founded the European Defence and Economic Community, immediately dubbed the 'United States of Europe' (USE) after Churchill's blueprint for it set out in his great Zurich speech of 19 September 1946, six months after Fulton.

Zurich was Europe's equivalent of Lincoln's Gettysburg Address, just a bit longer. 'I wish to speak to you today about the tragedy of Europe,' are its famous opening words. 'This noble continent,' Churchill continued:

> comprising on the whole the fairest and the most cultivated

> regions of the earth, enjoying a temperate and equable climate, is the home of all the great parent races of the Western world. It is the foundation of Christian faith and ethics. It is the origin of most of the culture, arts, philosophy and science both of ancient and modern times. If Europe were once united in the sharing of its common inheritance there would be no limit to the happiness, prosperity and glory which its 300 million or 400 million people would enjoy.

It was essential, Churchill continued, for there to be 'a blessed act of oblivion' about the past, as Gladstone had said a generation earlier about Britain and Ireland. But it was the practical agenda of the speech that made it so significant, and paved the way for the Treaty of Paris. 'Why,' he asked, 'should there not be a European group which could give a sense of enlarged patriotism and common citizenship to the distracted peoples of this turbulent and mighty continent and why should it not take its rightful place with the other great groupings in shaping the destinies of men?' Every schoolchild knows the urgent concluding words: 'Time may be short. At present there is a breathing space. The cannons have ceased firing. The fighting has stopped. But the dangers have not stopped. If we are to form a United States of Europe, or whatever name or form it may take, we must begin now.'

For Churchill, steeped in realpolitik, there was another imperative driving the formation of the USE, beyond strengthening the Atlantic Alliance and Western Europe's democracies. The British Empire was disintegrating fast, and there was nothing

Churchill could do about it. In February 1947, he appointed Lord Mountbatten as Viceroy of India, hoping to stabilise British rule on a more democratic basis. But it proved impossible. Significantly, the treaty to establish a European union was signed three months after India became independent in August 1947. In Churchill's 'three circles' view of Britain's international position – the Atlantic Alliance, the Commonwealth and 'United Europe' – the European circle became steadily more important. Crucially, Britain's remaining and former colonies got preferential access to the new European market as a key element of the Treaty of Paris with France, Italy, the Benelux countries and Germany when it joined in 1949. The other six accepted this partly as the price for vital defence and security guarantees; partly because of Churchill's immense prestige and leadership; partly because their own smaller colonies also received special treatment; and partly because of Britain's continuing industrial ascendancy in the 1940s. Not until the mid-1950s did the economy of the rest of Europe revive sufficiently to be a major competitor to Britain.

Crucially, Churchill seized the mantle of European leadership while there was no European competitor. Had a government taken office in 1945 unprepared to lead in Europe – say a Labour government led by the Eurosceptics Clement Attlee and Ernest Bevin – then Britain might have missed this vital window of opportunity and been faced with the humiliating prospect of supplicating to join a Franco-German enterprise sometime after the mid-1950s. The consequence might have been an ongoing 'half-in half-out' identity crisis bedevilling British politics for decades, maybe even until the present day.

Churchill became founder Secretary General of the United States of Europe in 1949 by acclaim of the founding Congress of European Parliaments of the seven initial member states. Robert Schuman, the outgoing Prime Minister of France who had been passionately in favour of the creation of the USE, became his deputy. He was succeeded as British Prime Minister by the strongly pro-European Harold Macmillan, who had made his name as post-war minister of housing before becoming Foreign Secretary in succession to Sir Anthony Eden. Eden ostensibly retired because of ill health; but behind the scenes, he had tried but failed to rally Tory ministers and MPs against Churchill on the sovereignty issue, in the early stages of the negotiations with Schuman on the Treaty of Paris.

Macmillan narrowly won the 1950 election, which led to the retirement of the veteran Labour leader Clement Attlee. His successor, the opportunistically pro-European Labour rising star, Harold Wilson, went on to win the 1954 election, and made his mark with the creation of the National Health Service and a welfare state to rival Churchill's achievements in the fields of defence, trade and European unity.

Shortly before the end of his first European term in 1953, Churchill suffered a stroke and retired. On his final day in office, Konrad Adenauer, a year younger than Churchill and now in his stride as first Chancellor of West Germany, presented the Charlemagne Prize to Europe's victor of war and peace. 'Why is it that you, Sir Winston, became the champion for the European ideal?' he asked rhetorically. 'I believe this can be explained from two human qualities that also are the requisite qualities for statesmanship: greatness of thought, depth of feeling.'

• • •

Maybe something like this would have happened if Churchill had shaped the peace as well as the war in the 1940s and early 1950s. Maybe not. But it is plausible – all the speeches and people are for real, and so are most of the treaties, with some changes of dates – and it goes some way to explaining what in fact happened. The European ideal and European cooperation, largely stimulated by Churchill, flowered on mainland Europe in the late 1940s and 1950s, ultimately in the Treaty of Rome in 1957, yet Britain stood apart until Macmillan – one of Churchill's closest pro-European lieutenants in the 1940s – finally made his 'if you can't beat them, join them' decision to apply for membership in 1961.

The following essays by Rachel Reeves on Attlee and David Dutton on Eden emphasise their deep Euroscepticism. Attlee created Churchill's inheritance, including the decision to stand completely apart from the European Coal and Steel Community, six months before Churchill became Prime Minister for the second time. Eden was his Foreign Secretary and heir apparent, with the expectation that he would succeed in short order and much sooner than actually happened (April 1955). Eden's view of 'European union' is summed up in his scribbled note on an early Foreign Office memorandum: 'Strasbourg [the Council of Europe] was always a misfortune; it is now nearly a calamity.'

Churchill in his prime was not hemmed in by either his predecessors or his colleagues. But by 1951, he was on thc wane, physically as much as politically. 'He was tired and his one big idea was a summit with Russia,' said his friend and protégé Bob Boothby. Believing he had only months in office, and that preventing the Korean War becoming another world conflagration was his one last mission, he soft peddled on European union, not least because it would only further antagonise Stalin.

A tantalising concluding thought. The notion of Churchill as first Secretary General of the European Union is not a flight of fantasy: it was there at the time. 'If I were ten years younger,' Churchill told his wife shortly after losing office in 1945, 'I might be the first President of the United States of Europe.'

The idea came up repeatedly in the early deliberations of the Council of Europe, Churchill's creation. In a dramatic debate on a defence union in 1950, the former French Prime Minister Pierre Reynaud – to whom in 1940 Churchill had made his proposal for a full Anglo-French union to avoid France falling to Hitler – pointed to Churchill as the man suited to be 'minister for war for Europe' in the face of the growing Russian menace. In the historian Felix Klos's account, 'Churchill saw no reason to dismiss the idea out of hand and smiled kindly in Reynaud's direction when the translation came through his headset.'

And there was a Treaty of Paris. It was signed in 1951, not 1948 as it might have been with Churchillian leadership. It inaugurated the European Coal and Steel Community, which became the European Community six years later. These are its remarkable opening words:

THE PRESIDENT OF THE FEDERAL REPUBLIC OF GERMANY, HIS ROYAL HIGHNESS THE PRINCE ROYAL OF BELGIUM, THE PRESIDENT OF THE FRENCH REPUBLIC, THE PRESIDENT OF THE ITALIAN REPUBLIC, HER ROYAL HIGHNESS THE GRAND DUCHESS OF LUXEMBOURG, HER MAJESTY THE QUEEN OF THE NETHERLANDS,

CONSIDERING that world peace can be safeguarded only by creative efforts commensurate with the dangers that threaten it,

CONVINCED that the contribution which an organized and vital Europe can make to civilization is indispensable to the maintenance of peaceful relations,

RECOGNIZING that Europe can be built only through practical achievements which will first of all create real solidarity, and through the establishment of common bases for economic development,

ANXIOUS to help, by expanding their basic production, to raise the standard of living and further the works of peace,

RESOLVED to substitute for age old rivalries the merging of their essential interests; to create, by establishing an economic community, the basis for a broader and deeper community among peoples long divided by bloody conflicts; and to lay the foundations for institutions which will give direction to a destiny henceforward shared,

HAVE DECIDED to create a EUROPEAN COAL AND STEEL COMMUNITY

Churchill could have written it. Just one thing was missing: 'His Majesty the King of the United Kingdom of Great Britain and Northern Ireland.'

CHAPTER 2

CLEMENT ATTLEE

RACHEL REEVES

'There would be no national planning, except under the guise of Continental planning. We shall not be able to deal with our own problems; we shall not be able to build up the country in the way we want to do.'

ATTLEE ON MACMILLAN'S APPLICATION TO JOIN THE EUROPEAN COMMUNITY IN 1962

Clement Attlee was Labour's great internationalist Prime Minister. He was Churchill's partner in wartime coalition and understood the need to stand defiant against Nazism. His government played a key role in the founding of NATO, the United Nations and the Council of Europe, as well as organising the European Recovery Programme (the 'Marshall Plan'). How, then, are we to understand this internationalist and champion of liberal institutions who was, for the first twenty years of its existence, vehemently opposed to British membership in the various iterations of the European Community?

Two aspects of Attlee's thought explain this. On the one hand, his preference for the Commonwealth as an ally, out of conviction and widely held perceptions of British economic and geopolitical interest at the time. On the other, he felt a strong commitment to parliamentary sovereignty and was unwilling to see this compromised. This attitude was born both of Attlee's socialism, which revolved around a belief in the need for state planning by elected representatives, and of his conservatism on questions of Britain's former empire and its historic parliamentary institutions.

Attlee's biographer John Bew says that on taking office Attlee and his Foreign Secretary Ernest Bevin faced three 'unavoidable, uncomfortable and interconnected realities'. These were, respectively, Britain's newfound economic and military dependence on the United States; the growing assertiveness of the USSR and the potential threat posed to British interests and security both in Europe and in the Eastern Mediterranean, North Africa and the Middle East; and the financial, political and moral unsustainability of empire. In this context, Attlee's interest in the question of European integration was limited. On one occasion, Attlee complained to Hugh Dalton about the excessively negative tone of a Labour Party pamphlet on the European Coal and Steel Community (ECSC), signed off by Labour's NEC – despite the fact that Attlee had been present at the meeting and his 'sole contribution had been to demand insertion of a sentence requiring protection for the horticultural industry!' For

Roger Liddle, this showed that 'he hadn't thought the subject of European unity important enough to justify him reading the document thoroughly'. As another Attlee biographer, Kenneth Harris, wrote, while 'on other major issues of foreign policy he dominated the party', when it came to European integration, 'he was not enthusiastic … but not unhelpful.'

To understand Attlee's policy on Europe, we should pay close attention not only to Attlee's own words and actions, but those of Ernest Bevin, who shared a relationship so close that, in Bew's words, 'to those outside government they seemed to convey complete unanimity on foreign affairs'. Despite Attlee's own apparent lack of interest, the European question loomed large throughout the period, climaxing at the tail end of Attlee's premiership with the formation of the European Coal and Steel Community (ECSC). Attlee's government was the first to decide not to pursue entry. It would be more than two decades until Britain joined what was by then widely known as the common market.

Hard economics were vital to this. The historian Robert Saunders argues that Britain's reticence about participating in European integration in the immediate post-war years relates to the way its immediate economic interests were understood. In the years after 1945, Europe did not look like Britain's key trading partner. A far greater proportion of British trade was with the Commonwealth than with the ECSC's original six member states, through to the first half of the 1950s. Britain appeared to be economically self-sufficient. In 1947, Britain exported five times as much as France and as much as all the future 'Six' combined. As late as 1951, British industrial production was still roughly equivalent to that of France and West Germany put together.

Meanwhile, the experience of war and fascism meant that the Six did not appear especially stable allies, and to integrate with their economies would have been to compromise imperial preference. As Stafford Cripps, Attlee's first President of the Board of Trade and later Chancellor, told the Cabinet, Britain 'could not integrate its economy into that of Europe in any way which would prejudice the discharge of its responsibilities towards the Commonwealth and the rest of the sterling area'. The UK was still at the centre of the Commonwealth universe, while being economically, politically and geographically at the periphery of Europe. Bevin reported that 'the United Kingdom – because of its overseas connexions – could never become an entirely European country'. It is this context that is most important in understanding the Attlee government's response to the question of European integration.

Attlee's political as well as economic priorities lay with the Commonwealth. Attlee had a strong emotional and personal bond with the Commonwealth, as Britain's club of colonies and ex-colonies became after Indian Independence in 1949. Haileybury, his Hertfordshire public school, had been the East India Company's training school and morphed into a public school with a mission for imperial service, and the young, idealistic 'Clem' went from Haileybury to Oxford in its imperial heyday. Bew argues that Attlee was motivated 'more than anyone else in his government' by the conviction that the old British Empire, that of Queen Victoria and the Diamond Jubilee, had come to an end, and should not be supported beyond its natural lifespan. Nonetheless, he saw the new Commonwealth as a real and vital political and economic bloc, not just a fig leaf for imperial decline.

For many on the left, a British-led Commonwealth was appealing as an alternative bloc to the United States and to the totalitarian Soviet Union. Indeed, the term 'Commonwealth' had left-wing connotations, being grounded in Britain's own radical and socialist traditions, to which Attlee was highly sensitised.

Attlee believed that the Commonwealth made Britain fundamentally different from other Western European countries. In the sole, short passage in his autobiography, *As It Happened*, that addressed the question of Europe, Attlee wrote that 'Britain has never regarded herself as just a European power. Her interests are world-wide. She is the heart of a great Commonwealth, and tends to look outwards from Europe, though maintaining a close interest in all that goes on in that Continent.'

Later in his life, as the House of Lords debated the Macmillan government's first application for British entry into the European Community in 1962, Attlee argued that the idea of an integrated Europe was 'historically looking backward and not forward … to the Holy Roman Empire. We never belonged to the Holy Roman Empire, and we never belonged to the reactionary organisation after 1815. We have always looked outward, out to the new world; and today, we look out to the new world and to Asia and Africa. I think that integration with Europe is a step backward.'

Warning the House of Commons of the potential for German dominance over the organisation, he opposed joining the ECSC in June 1950 on the grounds that 'by marrying into Europe, we are marrying a whole family of ancient prejudices and ancient troubles, and I would much rather see an Atlantic organisation. I would much rather work for the world organisation.' Attlee's vision of Europe was shaped by a lifetime dominated by war and the conflicting colonial ambitions of Europe's great powers. It is unsurprising that he looked beyond Europe for a hopeful vision of the future.

Attlee's constitutional conservatism was also an important factor. The historian and Labour MP Jon Cruddas has argued that Attlee's romanticism and idealism fed into his belief in the superiority of British institutions, including Parliament and the monarchy, in nurturing British values and virtue. The corollary was seeing patriotism itself as a virtue-representing loyalty to the institutions of the country, the 'emotion of every free-thinking Briton,' as Attlee described it.

Saunders notes, in his book on the 1975 referendum and its antecedents, that, unlike their European neighbours, 'The British did not have to rebuild their institutions at the war's end, or their sense of their own identity; indeed, the British state and its parliamentary institutions emerged from the conflict with their prestige and legitimacy enhanced.' The model of socialism articulated in the 1945 manifesto was based around a strong faith in parliamentary democracy: 'The idea that concentrations of economic power should be under the direction of a democratic Parliament was central to post-war social democracy in Britain, whose national institutions had not been tarnished by the experience of totalitarianism.' Also in his June 1950 speech in the Commons against membership of the ECSC, Attlee was categoric that a Labour government could not accept that 'the most vital economic forces of this country should be handed over to an authority that is utterly undemocratic and is responsible to nobody'. His view had not changed by the time of his Lords speech against Macmillan's EU application in November 1962, when he warned that:

> if the designs behind the common market are carried out, we are bound to be affected in every phase of our national life. There would be no national planning, except under the guise of Continental planning. We shall not be able to deal with our own problems; we shall not be able to build up the country in the way we want to do.

Put bluntly, Attlee believed the sacrifice of power over the economy that the ECSC and then the common market entailed would make it impossible to deliver socialism. Parliamentarism was central to Attlee's politics and those of the post-war Labour Party. This commitment shaped the *kind* of European integration that the party could support. As a 1950 Labour Party document put it, Labour 'could never accept any commitments which limited its own or others' freedom to pursue democratic socialism'.

However, Attlee's thinking was more complex than his approach to the ECSC might suggest. Where urgent imperatives were involved, with which he agreed, Attlee engaged in European cooperation of the closest kind, particularly on defence. Nor was he precious about 'parliamentary sovereignty', or even Cabinet government, in such circumstances. The highly secretive process for the development of Britain's first nuclear deterrent, shielded from most of the Cabinet, not just Parliament, is one instance. Equally far-reaching were the defence commitments, and limitations on independent national decision-making, involved in NATO. Long before the North Atlantic Treaty established NATO in 1949, Attlee and Bevin signed defence treaties with France and the Benelux countries which gave unconditional guarantees to go to war if they were attacked. Bevin at this stage thought Truman's administration too weak on Stalin. These kinds of unlimited commitments were precisely what Chamberlain had been resisting until the final showdown with Hitler in 1939.

It was because of the growing Soviet and communist threat across Europe, west as much as east, that in January 1948 Bevin came in belatedly behind Churchill and supported the creation of a 'Western Union'. He called it a 'spiritual union', rooted in 'the basic freedoms and ethical principles for which we all stand'. Bevin said this was intended to be 'a real positive reorganisation of the West, and not [to] give any impression that we were simply preparing for defence'.

Bevin's move grew out of his intense concern for the democratic stability of Western Europe. Defence guarantees weren't enough. Bevin was very opposed to the Popular Front governments, including communists, that took office in France and Italy in the immediate aftermath of war. He put huge pressure on the Italian Socialists to break with the communists, which was one of the first episodes that led to the Left Tribune attacks on Labour foreign policy. Hence, too, support for the Marshall Plan. Arguably Bevin's mistake was not to agree to the creation of an international mechanism for the management of the Marshall Plan. His opposition to this annoyed the Truman administration, which backed the ECSC proposal which might otherwise never have seen the light of day.

Attlee to some extent rationalised his approach as the difference between internationalism and supranationalism. He made this distinction in the Commons in 1950, when he explained his government's willingness to pool British sovereignty as part of the Atlantic Charter and the United Nations, stressing that in each of these instances:

> that surrender [of sovereignty] is made to a responsible body, a body of people responsible to Parliaments, not to an irresponsible body appointed by no one and responsible to no one. That is the special need for the use of that word, which I do not like particularly, but it does indicate the difference between what is international and what is 'supranational'.

This distinction is debatable. NATO and the ECSC, as the latter developed into the European Community with a national veto by member governments within the Council of Ministers, arguably weren't that different as international organisations. But the significant point is that Attlee, in the context of the post-war situation, sought to justify one form of internationalism (on defence) while rejecting it on another (economic regulation). Hence it was that within months of founding NATO, Attlee and Bevin refused to participate in discussions about the formation of the ECSC following the publication of the Schuman Plan. The Cabinet agreed they could not participate on these terms as 'no British government could be expected to accept such a commitment without having had any opportunity to assess the consequences which it might involve for our key industries, our export trade and our level of employment'. In a 1951 paper to Cabinet, Attlee set out the government's position in declining to join the ECSC:

> We are willing to play an active part in all forms of European cooperation on an intergovernmental basis but cannot surrender our freedom of decision and action to any supranational authority. We are quite ready to encourage Continental countries who feel disposed to adopt such plans and in the case of the Schuman Plan have declared our wish to be closely associated with any Authority that may be set up under it.

But even here, Attlee did not close the door entirely on enhanced forms of European economic and political cooperation. He stated instead of the ECSC a preference for an increased role for the Council of Europe, as 'the focal point of the European integration movement'.

While this logic made some sense at the time, the final structure of the ECSC in fact met many of the 'supranational' concerns. The Dutch ultimately insisted on the creation of a

Council of Ministers above the ECSC's 'High Authority' (which was to become the European Commission), which would need to give final assent to policy formulated by the Authority.

Some of Attlee's strongest objections were therefore against an *idea* of the Community which never existed. These concerns, however, extended beyond Attlee and Bevin to much of the Labour movement. Of the Schuman Plan, Attlee's Home Secretary Herbert Morrison famously remarked that 'the Durham miners will never wear it'. As the historian Michael Newman explains, while this 'might appear quite trivial', it in fact reflected the government's sensitivity to the position of the National Union of Mineworkers: 'Morrison … was deeply conscious of the fact that the ownership and control of the coal industry was a crucial issue in the Miners' Union.' Conscious of the resentment generated by the conduct of mine owners throughout the post-war period, especially following the general strike of 1926, Labour's leading figures were 'aware that anything which even *appeared* to undermine the recent nationalisation of coal would precipitate serious opposition within the party and the trade union movement'.

Another noteworthy aspect of Attlee's involvement with Europe after 1945 is the reconstruction of West Germany. Bevin took a leading role in securing a model for the German economy based around decentralised industry and co-determination – workers' participation in the running of industry. Influenced by wariness of the role of a central German state, by French and American opposition to nationalisation of coal and steel in the Ruhr and by growing support for the policy within the

German labour movement, Bevin played an instrumental role in securing the introduction of a system of co-determination between management and trade unions. This represented a significant shift from some of the ideas prevalent among the Allies in wartime, which held that the only way to deal with post-war Germany was to flatten its industry. The introduction of co-determination, alongside the rapid economic recovery facilitated by the Marshall Plan, set the scene for the enviable success of Germany's social market economy since.

Whereas in West Germany, a new system was built which entwined workers' interests with the company's fate, in Britain, nationalisation took a different course. The Labour Party *excluded* workers from the nationalised industries in the UK, allowing them to be run by Whitehall and not by the workers. Only on the Continent could Bevin really achieve his vision of socialism which, in the words of his biographer Alan Bullock, meant 'something more than planning and public ownership; it meant a change in the status of the worker, the end of that exclusion from responsibility, the stigma of inferiority, which he had always regarded as the key to improving industrial relations'.

The British model left itself open to attack from both left and right and could not outlive the 1980s. By contrast, the German model has continued to thrive and played a key part in the resilience of the German economy in the wake of the 2008 financial crisis. As Frances O'Grady, the General Secretary of the Trades Union Congress, argued in her Attlee Memorial Lecture of 2013, Britain had suffered from the legacy of its 'failure to seize the opportunity of the European model of co-determination and industrial democracy'. Today, as we attempt to build an alternative to Britain's failing economic model, with growing inequality and low productivity, we might look again to the German example.

• • •

By 1962, when the Macmillan government made the first, unsuccessful application for Britain's entry into the common market, Attlee was almost eighty years old and a member of the House of Lords. At this point – perhaps because he had hardened in his views or perhaps because he no longer felt bound to speak with the caution of a Prime Minister – he was considerably more strident in his opposition to entry. These arguments were often characterised by glib references to the war. For instance, he told one newspaper that 'we beat Germany and we beat Italy, and we have saved France and Belgium and Holland. I never see why we should go crawling to them'. On another occasion, he is said to have remarked, when asked about joining the Six that 'I seem to remember that we spent a lot of blood and treasure during the war rescuing four of them from the other two'.

Despite these provocations, Attlee's arguments against entry into 1962 were much the same as his reasoning had been over a decade before. Aware that the political tide had turned, he conceded to the Lords that 'I am afraid I shall be accused of being old-fashioned and out of date, but I still think that for this country a degree of flexibility is desirable. The common market means a great deal of rigidity [in foreign policy].' It remained crucial that 'we have never before tied ourselves up so closely that our whole economic life depends on the work of people other than ourselves'. Despite his changed tone, his arguments remained largely the same: that he was 'prepared to give up sovereignty to the world, but not to a selected number of countries', particularly countries among whom 'no one … has been very successful in running parliamentary institutions', and still he objected to a supranational institution in which 'the whole of the planning is done by officials [and] the Ministers come in at a later stage'. The same themes – a deep faith in Britain's institutions, a preference for the Commonwealth and scepticism about the reliability of the Western European powers as allies, and a belief that socialism in Britain must be achieved through the exercise of power by Britain's Parliament over the economy – animated Attlee's opposition in 1962 much as they had in the late 1940s.

In many ways, Attlee's world seems a long way away. As Bew suggests, if we are to learn lessons from his great reforming government, it is more in terms of its ethos than in its specific policy programme. We cannot go back to 1945, in foreign policy terms as much as in any other respect. Nor should we wish to. When Attlee died, Britain still had an empire and we should be proud of the role that Labour governments played in ending colonial rule over much of the world. But there are also profound challenges that any social-democratic government faces today which Attlee did not have to take into account to the same extent, notably those challenges we associate with a globalised economy and powerful multinational corporates.

In the aftermath of war, Britain's institutions and its political class emerged strengthened in the political and popular imagination. Today we have lived through a decade of public distrust in our institutions, from Parliament to the media and the banks. Our political system and economic model are no longer able to deliver for people and they are not trusted to serve anyone but insiders. Our global role is unclear. It is a historical irony that Britain's initial decision not to enter the European Community was born of faith in our institutions. Our decision to leave the European Union has drawn above all on a catastrophic collapse of faith in our institutions.

There are lessons we can learn from Attlee. His partnership with Bevin was absolutely central to the construction of the post-war liberal international order which still endures today. They were politically bold in restructuring and building from the ground up, domestic and international institutions. Today we need some of that boldness of action and vision to meet the challenges of the broken neoliberal economic model, man-made climate change, and a volatile and unpredictable international order. John Bew describes so well Attlee's 'unobtrusive progressive patriotism – built on a sense of rights and duties, a malleable civic code rather than a legal writ, with its emphasis on the "common wealth" above individual self-fulfilment'. This ethos can still offer lessons to Labour about how to bring a fragmented country together.

Our task in the decade ahead is to build an economy which delivers a profound and lasting redistribution of power and wealth from capital to labour. And so we should also learn from

Attlee's mistakes. His beliefs about Europe were sometimes based on wrong assumptions. They had been shaped by the world of empire and the Second World War, not by the new, post-war world Britain was entering. The relative importance of the Commonwealth to Britain's economy declined. Western Europe made a remarkable political and economic recovery. Britain's economic performance declined relative to its Western European neighbours. Attlee found himself an isolated voice in opposition to entry. On some level, he probably suspected as much. As Prime Minister, he told one group of younger MPs: 'I want you to go to this new thing called the Council of Europe. I don't know much about it, but in *your* time, you'll *have* to.'

CHAPTER 3

ANTHONY EDEN

DAVID DUTTON

'Europe will be your revenge.'

CHANCELLOR KONRAD ADENAUER TO FRENCH PRIME MINISTER GUY MOLLET AFTER EDEN 'ABANDONED' FRANCE DURING THE 1956 SUEZ CRISIS

Notwithstanding its brevity (twenty-one months) and overwhelming focus on the Suez Crisis, Anthony Eden's premiership witnessed some of the most significant landmarks on the road to European integration. Less than two months after Eden took over from Winston Churchill in 10 Downing Street, the Foreign Ministers of the six members of the European Coal and Steel Community met in the town of Messina on the north-east point of Sicily. It was a somewhat unpromising venue, determined in large part by the electoral requirements of the Italian Foreign Minister Gaetano

Martino, for the hugely important deliberations that subsequently took place. Because the meeting coincided with the Old Bailey trial of the so-called Messina brothers, for most Britons, wrote Hugo Young, 'mention of Messina inspired only thoughts of prostitution and extortion by oily Italians running a corner of London gang-land'. Yet the resulting talks focused on a possible commitment 'to work for the establishment of a united Europe by the development of common institutions, the gradual fusion of national economies, the creation of a common market and the gradual harmonisation of ... social policies'.

Thereafter, in marked contrast to the agonising death throes of the proposed European Defence Community (EDC) between 1950 and 1954, events moved with almost dizzying speed. Out of Messina grew the discussions of the Spaak Committee, which centred on the twin goals of a customs union and a European atomic energy authority, at which Britain maintained low-level and only temporary representation. Then on 25 March 1957, less than three months after Eden's resignation, the six European powers signed the Treaty of Rome, setting up the European Economic Community (EEC). 'Europe' was born – and Britain was not a part of it.

But Eden's importance in this story derives not merely from a coincidence of timing, with the Europeans making their decisive moves on his prime ministerial watch. Between October 1951 and April 1955 he had served as Foreign Secretary under Churchill and, for six years before that, he had been the Conservative Party's chief spokesman on foreign affairs during the period of post-war Labour government. He was thus at, or near, the seat of power from the first stirrings of the European movement in the late 1940s until a matter of weeks before their triumphal fruition in March 1957.

By the early 1960s, a new elite consensus had begun to develop which insisted not only that Britain's destiny lay in Europe, but also that in the first dozen years after the Second World War Britain had thrown away a unique opportunity to seize the leadership of the European movement and shape it in the country's own interests. Now largely withdrawn from public life, Eden quickly assumed the role of scapegoat. With Churchill an iconic figure for Euro-enthusiasts, it was easy to attribute his failure to redirect British foreign policy after returning to office in 1951 to the negative influence of his Foreign Secretary and ultimate successor. First in the political memoirs of his Conservative contemporaries and then in the early academic historiography, Eden's baleful role was sketched out. By 1986, Roy Jenkins, politician and historian, and carrying the added authority of a former President of the European Commission, could sum up the by then accepted wisdom on Eden's culpability: 'More than anyone else [Eden] was responsible for allowing Europe to be made without us in the crucial years from 1951 to 1956.'

Eden was unusually sensitive about his historical reputation. His volume of memoirs covering the years 1951–57, published out of chronological sequence in 1960 in order to cover the eventuality of his own early death, was written essentially as a preventive strike in a correctly anticipated historiographical battle over Suez. His skilfully crafted, but carefully sanitised account gave

Eden his chance to place his version of the affair on the record. His treatment of Europe, by contrast, appeared bland and uncontroversial, for Eden felt no need to be either apologetic or defensive over this issue. The meeting at Messina merited just one passing reference in the nearly 600 pages of *Full Circle*. The later criticism of his European policy took him by surprise and provoked considerable anger. It was a case, Eden commented with acidic distaste in a private letter of 1969, of what 'is called the benefit of hindsight, I believe'. Of the account contained in the memoirs of Lord Kilmuir, who as David Maxwell-Fyfe had been Home Secretary from 1951 to 1954, he was especially scathing in a private letter of 1964:

> The story about EDC [European Defence Community] and the alleged differences [in 1951] is a complete fabrication. The evidence is simple enough. Kilmuir never opened his trap on the subject in Cabinet. If he had felt so strongly about my wickedness, why didn't he put in a paper or even resign instead of toadying Winston and myself with equal sycophancy?

For a while, Eden toyed with the possibility of legal action. More constructively, he engaged the young historian, Ben Pimlott, to examine his private archive and produce a paper on Britain's European policy in the early 1950s, designed to refute the arguments of his critics.

• • •

The government formed by Winston Churchill after the Conservative victory in the general election of October 1951 evoked some elements of the same Prime Minister's wartime coalition. In particular, Eden as Foreign Secretary returned to the post he had held with distinction for most of the Second World War. Yet Eden's position and the relationship between the two men were significantly changed. At almost seventy-seven years of age, Churchill no longer had the strength or stamina to intervene actively in all areas of government. In relation to foreign affairs, his selective focus was very much fixed on relations between the great powers, of which, he believed, the United Kingdom remained indubitably one. Indeed, the quest for a summit conference with Eisenhower and Stalin and his successors became the abiding mission of his final administration. Europe, by contrast, was a secondary affair that could be safely left in the Foreign Secretary's experienced hands. It is, though, certainly true that many expected Churchill's return to office to occasion a change in Britain's approach to the European movement.

Conservative Europhiles had perhaps paid too much attention to Churchill's rhetorical flourishes of the late 1940s and not enough to the accompanying small print. However, the proposition that Eden took advantage of the Prime Minister's waning powers to divert him from his chosen course is unconvincing. The latter's earlier pronouncements, inspiring but ill-defined, had created expectations that he never tried to fulfil when restored to office. In a paper on 'United Europe', which the Prime Minister himself circulated at the end of November 1951, he emphasised that he was not opposed to the idea of federation, provided it came about naturally and gradually. But 'I never thought that Britain or the British Commonwealth should, either individually or collectively, become an integral part of a European Federation and have never given the slightest support to the idea.'

Such prime ministerial pronouncements provide the context for the supposed divergence between Eden and Maxwell-Fyfe in their respective statements on 28 November on the so-called Pleven Plan for a European Defence Community. On 24 October, the French Prime Minister had suggested that West German rearmament should only take place within a supranational framework. The proposed European Defence Community would have a European Defence minister answerable to a European Assembly, a European Defence Council of Ministers and a single European defence budget. With memories of world war still fresh, the French aim was to 'spin a cocoon of supranational restraints around Western Germany from which it could not escape'.

Speaking in Strasbourg, Maxwell-Fyfe welcomed European initiatives for closer integration, while signalling Britain's reluctance to move beyond the realm of intergovernmental cooperation. A few hours later in Rome, Eden declared that Britain would never join a supranational Defence Community and that the most that could be contemplated was 'association' with such a body. There was a difference of emphasis here and the following weeks did see efforts by Harold Macmillan and others to sound a more positive note than the Foreign

Secretary had managed. But divisions within the government and party were never as deep as later suggested, and the idea that Eden had single-handedly destroyed any lingering hope that Britain could still seize the leadership seems fanciful. Most ministers accepted the thrust of an important policy statement that emerged in mid-December from the Permanent Under-Secretary's Committee inside the Foreign Office:

> The United Kingdom cannot seriously contemplate joining in European integration. Apart from geographical and strategic considerations, Commonwealth ties and the special position of the United Kingdom as the centre of the sterling area, we cannot consider submitting our political and economic system to supranational institutions ... But while it is neither practicable nor desirable for the United Kingdom to join the integration movement, there would seem to be advantage in encouraging the movement without taking part in it. This is, in fact, the policy which the United Kingdom is now following.

Eden's ideas on Europe were in the mainstream of contemporary thought. By no criteria could he be described as a 'Little Englander'. He was well travelled, not least as a result of a total of more than ten years as Foreign Secretary. No other leading British politician could claim to have met and negotiated with Hitler, Mussolini and Stalin. More positively, he was born into and deeply influenced by European culture. Unlike the majority of his successors, he was fluent in French and competent enough in German. He delighted in reading and rereading

Proust in the original. Brought up in a house containing works by Degas, Corot and Murillo, his own artistic tastes were, by the standards of the time, advanced and, on a relatively limited budget, he acquired works by artists such as Derain, Braque and Picasso. As an undergraduate he had delivered a well-received paper on the art of Cezanne. It was perhaps unsurprising that this genuine Francophile had proved a doughty champion of France's claims to the restoration of great power status at the end of the Second World War.

But Eden's understanding of history convinced him of the strength of British nationalism, which, he believed, 'could never be buried in some alien construct'. He was also a strong supporter of the Commonwealth. 'For us', he stressed in his adoption speech for the 1950 general election, 'the Commonwealth and Empire must always be a first consideration'. Nearly seventy years on, it is easy to dismiss such thinking as myopic. The bonds that held the white dominions, in particular, close to the 'mother country' would rapidly weaken. But Eden's thinking was by no means eccentric. Indeed, it was part of a cross-party consensus that scarcely merited further discussion and which contemporary statistics appeared to support. From 1950 to 1954, the Commonwealth accounted for 49 per cent of Britain's imports and took 54 per cent of her exports. In addition, though Eden was never as starry-eyed as Churchill about the 'special relationship', he regarded the maintenance of the Atlantic Alliance and of America's commitment to the defence of Western Europe as the indispensable foundation of British foreign policy. Rather like Churchill with his concept of three interlinked circles, Eden saw Britain's ongoing great power status resting upon 'three unities' – the Empire and Commonwealth, the Anglo-American alliance and relations with Western Europe. And again, as with Churchill, the last was also the least important of the three. Granted the state of the post-war European economies, it could hardly have been otherwise. Notwithstanding the ravages of world war, all relevant economic indices placed the British economy comfortably ahead of those of her Continental neighbours. On these bases Britain remained a great power in the early 1950s, with vital interests around the globe, even though the key measure in this assessment was increasingly commitments and obligations rather than resources.

Such thinking shaped Eden's response to the proposed EDC. In Cabinet in February 1952, he reminded his colleagues that the 'long-term aim of the European Defence Community [was] to pave the way for a European federation'. As such, British membership was out of the question. Two and a half years later, after the project had collapsed, his attitude was the same. To the House of Commons he declared:

> The whole essence of EDC lay in its supranational character, leading to a federal structure for Europe. That might be a good thing or it might not; I am not prepared to argue that. Some people were all for it and some were against it, but, so far, no party in this country has been willing to subscribe to that conception for ourselves.

In fact, Eden's stance towards the EDC, providing it did not formally include Britain, had been more positive than this statement might seem to imply. He was always conscious of the value of Franco-German rapprochement to the maintenance of European peace and in any case 'it would not be right – or good policy – to try to stop the others' from following their inclinations, he wrote in a 1952 minute.

In no sense is it fair to claim that Eden set out to wreck Europe's supranational ambitions. Over the months that preceded the final rejection of EDC by France's Chamber of Deputies, he showed himself willing to make major concessions to secure its success, providing these fell short of the full pooling of British sovereignty. Underlying Eden's diplomacy was the knowledge that the United States placed considerable stress on EDC as the best – and perhaps the only – means of securing a West German contribution to the heavy costs of European defence. He took seriously the suggestion made by the American Secretary of State, John Foster Dulles, in December 1953, that EDC's collapse could trigger an 'agonising reappraisal' of the United States' commitment to the Continent and the possible substitution of 'peripheral defence'. As Eden told Lord Alexander, the British Minister of Defence: 'I think that we have got to think seriously what we can do to save the whole pan [because] the whole future of American support for Europe may turn on this.' By March 1954 he was looking for Cabinet approval for a commitment to maintain the current fighting capacity of UK forces on the Continent and to put a British armoured division under the command of an EDC corps and keep it there for as long as the Supreme Allied Commander in Europe deemed necessary. This was the sort of defence commitment from Britain which the French had sought since before the First World War and, as the historian Kevin Ruane notes, 'stretched the British policy of [mere] association to breaking point'.

Only when the French Chamber voted down the EDC proposal in August 1954 did Eden come forward with the sort of alternative plan which, if launched earlier, could well have been viewed merely as a spoiling mechanism. The weeks that followed were in many ways the highpoint of his diplomatic career. With energy and purpose he toured the capitals of the European Six and patiently overcame unhelpful interventions from Dulles and the French premier, Pierre Mendès-France. As chairman of the conference which met in London on 28 September he was in his element, combining the silky negotiating skills for which he was rightly renowned with a steely determination to prevail whenever the going got tough. Eden's solution allowed for the extension of the Brussels Pact of 1948, itself the precursor of NATO, to include West Germany and Italy. The expanded organisation became the Western European Union in 1955. The Allied occupation of West Germany would now end, allowing that country to recover its full sovereignty and become a member of NATO. To clinch the deal Eden offered to maintain four British divisions on the European mainland, together with a tactical airforce for as long as necessary, a further strengthening of the commitment offered a few months earlier when EDC was still on the table. Britain and the Six were thus joined in an intergovernmental, non-supranational body which Britain might logically expect to lead. Praise for the Foreign

Secretary's achievement was almost universal. There followed the Wateler Peace Prize from the Carnegie Foundation and the Order of the Garter from the Queen. Supposed Conservative Europhiles appeared satisfied. In the privacy of his diary, Macmillan recorded 'a *tremendous* triumph for Eden'. There was no qualifying statement that he would have preferred the now abandoned supranational option.

By the time Eden finally succeeded Churchill as Prime Minister in April 1955, it really did seem that the European movement was travelling in a direction congenial to Britain – towards unity rather than union. What Eden and the vast majority of his political generation failed to anticipate was the speed with which European federalists would recover from the setback of EDC, build on the achievements of the Coal and Steel Community and relaunch their integrationist programme. The French rejection of EDC led to understandable scepticism about the ability of the Six to make any further progress along supranational lines.

Eden's government clearly underestimated the importance of the gathering at Messina, as indicated by the dismissive comment of the Chancellor of the Exchequer, R. A. Butler, at an Organisation for European Economic Cooperation (OEEC) dinner. The Chancellor spoke of 'some archaeological excavations' at an old Sicilian town, in which Britain had not taken part. The British ambassador in Rome, while bettering Butler's attempt at humour, reported in comparable terms: 'The Messina conference did not arouse much enthusiasm in the Italian press which was fully occupied with the Sicilian election campaign.

According to my Dutch colleague it was not intended to achieve anything, but all the Foreign Ministers enjoyed their holiday in Taormina.'

The prevailing assumption in Whitehall was that Britain would be able to associate herself loosely with anything that might emerge from Europe, if only because the continuing mutual suspicions of France and Germany made a British presence desirable to both. In these circumstances, British representation on the resulting Spaak Committee by a Board of Trade official, Russell Bretherton, rather than a senior minister, probably created the desired impression. But Bretherton became concerned that the more Britain got involved in the committee's deliberations, the more she would appear committed to the ultimate outcome. The head of the British delegation to the OEEC was even more cautious, writing to Foreign Secretary Macmillan at the end of 1945:

> If it is not our intention to become members of the Common Market or be associated … it is far better to be outspoken at the outset … I would regard it as a fatal mistake to abandon our present status in order to become a member of a purely European grouping which by implication would require some abandonment of sovereignty.

This sort of thinking prompted the British government to distance itself from the Spaak Committee and Bretherton was withdrawn in early November. Eden's personal influence as Prime Minister is less evident than it had been as Foreign

Secretary. But his readiness to delegate responsibility to the Exchequer, the Foreign Office and the Board of Trade offers further evidence that he did not see himself as in any sense out of step with his senior Cabinet colleagues.

In a distinct change of policy, the government now sought much more actively than before to steer the Six away from supranationalism by promoting a British alternative to a common market in the form of a wider free trade area, based on the OEEC. If, as was widely believed, this was intended as an exercise in sabotage, it probably served merely to concentrate the minds of European federalists more purposefully on their chosen goal. Indeed, when the six heads of government prepared to meet in Brussels in June 1956 to start drafting a treaty, it was made clear that Britain could only be represented if she was prepared to negotiate on the basis of the Spaak Report, a stipulation that precluded British participation.

Plan 'G', as the British scheme became known, was soon overshadowed by Colonel Nasser's nationalisation of the Suez Canal Company on 26 July 1956. Eden's attention was now firmly fixed on the Middle East and not Europe. But a debate in the Commons just six weeks before Eden's final resignation is important for Macmillan's statement of the government's position: 'I do not believe that this House would ever agree to our entering arrangements which, as a matter of principle, would prevent our treating the great range of imports from the Commonwealth at least as favourably as those from the European countries.'

As Eden would recall in 1969, it had never been a case of 'tepid Europeans ... propounding policy and holding back colleagues who would have entered a customs union'. Albeit unknowingly, in these final weeks of his political career Eden probably made his greatest contribution to ultimate European union. The French bitterly resented the way in which the British government unilaterally ended the Suez expedition without reference to themselves. Once again, it seemed, France had been betrayed by Perfidious Albion. Almost certainly, this helped persuade her to abandon earlier hesitations and commit to a European destiny. As West Germany's Chancellor Konrad Adenauer was reported as saying to the French Prime Minister, Guy Mollet, 'Europe will be your revenge.'

• • •

Eden's career in frontline politics came to an abrupt end with his resignation in 1957. Yet the story of his association with the movement for European integration contains a brief but not insignificant postscript. According to W. E. Gladstone, 'former Prime Ministers are like untethered rafts drifting around harbours – a menace to shipping'. The history of Britain's relationship with the EEC and its successor, the European Union, provides plenty of evidence to support this contention. But the referendum campaign of 2016 also confirmed the importance of 'big names' and their potential to change popular opinion. Harold Macmillan was relatively fortunate that no major figure emerged to challenge his decision in 1961 to seek

British membership of the common market. 'I see no Disraeli among them,' he recorded, 'not even a Lord George Bentinck,' he confided to his diary. Notwithstanding Suez, Eden had the potential to fill this void. But his retirement from public life was more complete than that of any of his prime ministerial successors. His body had been permanently damaged by the series of major operations he underwent, beginning in 1953. Still under sixty at the time of his resignation, for a time he nurtured the hope that renewed good health might permit a return to active political life. But in 1961, he reconciled himself to the inevitable and accepted a peerage, taking a seat in the Lords (though rarely using it) as the Earl of Avon. Easily tired and subject without warning to a recurrence of the fevers that had begun with his botched gallstone operation in 1953, he seldom visited London and tried to escape the trials of the British winter whenever possible. So strong, however, were Eden's feelings on the matter that Macmillan's dramatic change of European policy did prompt a brief return to the political arena and certainly gave rise to vigorous activity in his private correspondence.

Eden's concerns remained essentially unchanged from the 1950s. In particular, the British public needed to consider the ultimate goals of the European movement before signing up to it. Strained metaphors about Britain 'missing the European bus' or 'letting the European train set off' without her have been the common currency of the debate for many years. If Eden were to board a European vehicle, he was first determined to know what its destination would be.

Towards the end of September 1962, Eden met privately with his former Cabinet colleague Oliver Lyttelton, now Lord Chandos. The two men agreed on the need to confront the issue of federalism head-on. 'The more I think of it', wrote Chandos to Eden after their meeting, 'the more certain I am that the country must be told about the possibility of federation quite openly and secondly I am equally sure that they would reject it.' But Chandos's concerns were largely assuaged following a meeting with Macmillan on 4 October. Macmillan insisted that the Treaty of Rome was restricted to economic matters and that, as a member of the EEC, Britain would be in a position to veto any moves towards a closer political structure. Eden, by contrast, remained unconvinced, writing to Chandos in October 1962:

> I myself doubt if the experiment of the Six can succeed without federation and I think it most probable that if we join the Six we shall be faced with that decision in a few years' time … I am sure that it must be federation in the sense of one Parliament, one foreign policy, one currency etc. So far as I can judge events on the Continent of Europe, I do not want to become part of such a federation.

Eden's most public contribution to the discussion of Britain's possible membership of the common market came in a House of Lords debate on 8 November 1962. He began with a careful consideration of the potential economic impact of British membership, highlighting the danger of Britain's Commonwealth partners being left without a market for their agricultural produce. In the economic sphere, Eden declared, 'What we may shortly have to decide is more important than any decision since the repeal of the Corn Laws.' On the political side 'it can be more important than any decision we have taken in history'. The European Commission had stated that progress towards economic union was progress towards political union. This was a 'confession of intent which we should be ostriches to ignore'. Like later Eurosceptics he insisted that those who had doubts about closer political unity did not contemplate or in any sense desire to turn their backs on Europe. He stated, 'What some of us find it difficult to visualise is the form which this closer political unity can now be expected to take. How much closer can we get to each other, and what will the process entail for the authority of Parliament in this country?'

Britain should not lightly forget her supreme legacy to Western civilisation – 'the art of self-government by a free people'. The countries of the Six had made shining contributions to the ideal of liberty, but had not shown the same loyalty to parliamentary democracy as Britain had.

In these circumstances, Eden concluded:

> It does not seem to me unreasonable or offensive to any country to ask that Her Majesty's government should make their position clear before they embark on negotiations which may lead to the acceptance of conditions intended by others to promote federation. This seems to me indispensable, if we have no intention of travelling the full way ourselves … What we

> must not do is to join any organisation without a full understanding of its implications and then find ourselves being swept further than we intended ... Better clarity now than recrimination a few years hence.

Eden's powerful speech was well received by many peers, including Attlee. In the event, Macmillan's initiative was destroyed not at Westminster but in France. The veto of President de Gaulle, announced on 14 January 1963, brought Britain's first application to join the European community to an ignominious end.

The quest for objective 'facts' and 'truth' regarding Britain's troubled relationship with Europe since the end of the Second World War remains elusive, suspended between an unknowable future and a counterfactual past. But Eden's contribution to this story merits respect. As one of his more perceptive biographers has put it, he 'was not some politician from a vanished age, struggling in vain against an integrationist flood tide in West Europe, let alone Britain'. Eden propounded a consistent, intellectually coherent and persuasive case for caution on the part of the British government in the face of long-term threats to the nation state. Arguments based upon possible economic advantage, used by Macmillan and Heath to persuade a sceptical public of the advantages of British participation, were for him not enough. He was concerned to address head-on the issue that, for him, really mattered – national sovereignty. 'All I am concerned about', he insisted in a letter to Chandos in 1962, 'is that the British people should know where they are going before they wake up and find themselves where they do not want to be.'

CHAPTER 4

HAROLD MACMILLAN

DAVID FABER

'I said that I thought the present position tragic ... [and] was there not a danger that if it went through, the position in ten years would be still worse? There would be a European Community which would dominate Europe and would be roughly equal to Hitler's Europe of 1940. If we stay out, we risk that German domination of Europe which we have fought two world wars to prevent.'

HAROLD MACMILLAN'S DIARY, AFTER CHURCHILL'S CABINET MEETING IN NOVEMBER 1951 WHICH DECIDED AGAINST CLOSER EUROPEAN ENGAGEMENT

In later life, in the course of a long retirement at his Sussex home Birch Grove, Harold Macmillan was fond of taking visitors to an outbuilding when giving a tour of the house. Rusting away in a corner, there still remained the specially purchased fridge, where supplies of President de Gaulle's rare blood group had been stored during his stay in November 1961. Unsurprisingly, the Macmillans' cook had baulked at the idea of the blood being stored in her own kitchen fridge. De Gaulle's terror of assassination attempts had also led to the macabre sight of his heavy-duty military cavalcade from Gatwick having both an ambulance and a car full of various surgeons sandwiched between the cars containing the principal protagonists.

It was not just the cook who was unimpressed: Birch Grove's head gamekeeper thought nothing of loudly interrupting a meeting between Macmillan and de Gaulle to complain about the effect the numerous secret service personnel traipsing around the woods would have on the following week's shooting. At least one journalist was bitten by a police dog (from the *Daily Mail* and in the behind) while trying to gain unauthorised access to the estate.

The air of tension outside echoed the mood of the talks taking place inside the house. Macmillan wanted to talk about UK entry to the European Economic Community (EEC), but de Gaulle was more preoccupied with the situation in Berlin where the Russians had closed the border and begun work on the Berlin Wall that August; there was no agreement on a concerted Anglo-French response and Macmillan described the talks on Europe as 'equally unproductive'.

• • •

By 1961, Macmillan and de Gaulle had known each other for more than twenty years. After an initial meeting in London in

1940, the two met again in Algiers in 1943; de Gaulle having moved his *La France Libre* headquarters there from London and Macmillan having been appointed by Churchill as his Minister Resident in the Mediterranean, with full Cabinet rank. As well as being tasked to maintain and improve Anglo-US relations at Allied headquarters, a further key aspect of Macmillan's role was to deal with the French on behalf of the British government and, in particular, to give greater credibility to de Gaulle's claims to become de facto French leader in exile, in place of the Americans' favoured candidate, General Henri Giraud, the French High Commissioner for North and West Africa.

The first responsibility to confront Macmillan on arrival in North Africa was the Casablanca Conference in January 1943, attended by Churchill, President Roosevelt, General Eisenhower and, reluctantly, de Gaulle. Macmillan quickly became the all-important go-between, his job to establish which of de Gaulle and Giraud would be most acceptable as the sole French leader in the eyes of the American hierarchy. Macmillan favoured de Gaulle, but his job was not made easy, either by the American delegation's obvious loathing for de Gaulle, or by the general's reluctance to allow himself to be put forward in the first place. However, Macmillan's persistence paid off and the conference, which had primarily been called to assess the overall progress and subsequent Allied strategy for the war in North Africa, was best remembered for the symbolic but reluctant handshake between de Gaulle and Giraud on the very last day.

The upshot of the Casablanca negotiations was the creation

that summer of the Comité Française de Libération Nationale (FCNL), jointly chaired by de Gaulle and Giraud – a diplomatic triumph for Macmillan, but also an early baptism of fire in dealing with de Gaulle. When the dust had settled, Macmillan wrote to de Gaulle that he had 'always valued very highly our acquaintance – or perhaps I may be allowed to call it friendship – and I feel certain that the role you have played during these three terrible years fits you to play a still greater one in the future'. De Gaulle replied in similarly enthusiastic terms; he had been touched by Macmillan's letter, was grateful for his positive interventions on behalf of the British government and greatly valued Macmillan's 'sympathy, which I also venture to call your friendship'.

In the summer of 1943, having survived a serous air crash at Algiers in February, Macmillan was given the job by Churchill of resolving the problem of the remnants of the French Vichy fleet, known as 'Force X', that had been immobilised in Alexandria harbour since June 1940 under Admiral René-Émil Godfroy, who remained loyal to Marshal Pétain and the Vichy government. Macmillan's task was to negotiate the return of these ships to the Allied cause, something he achieved with the requisite skill and diplomacy. His French equivalent in the negotiations was the diplomat Jean Monnet, who, since the fall of France, had so far spent the war in London and Washington, and had now been posted to Algiers by Roosevelt as a senior member of the FCNL, effectively a provisional French government-in-waiting.

Monnet, later to be known as 'the father of Europe', had already outlined his ambitious vision for a post-war united

Europe to leaders in both London and Washington. He now worked closely with Macmillan to make a success of the FCNL; the two men forged a close friendship and Monnet enthused Macmillan with his grand plan for a Europe that would achieve both economic and political federation.

For Macmillan, the experience of trying to win over de Gaulle, while keeping both the Americans and Churchill happy, was one that he would recall vividly twenty years later when negotiating with the French President. Macmillan confided to his diary that Churchill thought him 'much too pro-French' and sympathetic to de Gaulle. The late historian Peter Mangold quotes Churchill's view of de Gaulle at the time: 'an egoist, self-regarding, excessively proud, irrational, self-important, he reduces everything to himself. Not very loyal, anti-English, anti-American. He cultivates and furthers a sentiment of Anglophobia everywhere.' When de Gaulle took his leave of Foreign Secretary Anthony Eden before flying to Algiers in May 1943, Eden complained that he had caused the British a greater headache than all their other European allies put together. 'I don't doubt it,' replied de Gaulle with a wry smile. 'France is a great power.' Macmillan had, says Mangold, 'played a central role in helping to mediate one of the most important political agreements in twentieth-century French history'.

In the immediate aftermath of the Second World War, Macmillan, in spite of his time in North Africa and Italy, was still perceived as more of a specialist in domestic and economic matters than in foreign policy. Although described by the *Oxford Dictionary of National Biography* as, by now, 'one of

Britain's best-equipped, all-round Tory politicians', he lost his Stockton seat in the landslide Labour Party election triumph of July 1945, but returned to Parliament just a few months later through a Bromley by-election. Macmillan now recognised that if he was to reach the very top of the political tree he needed to widen his knowledge and boost his reputation in the field of foreign affairs. He began to contribute more frequently to foreign affairs debates in the House, and a well-reported 1947 visit to India boosted his profile still further. However, Macmillan's biographer D. R. Thorpe tells us that Macmillan returned from India in a deeply pessimistic mood. He bemoaned the chaotic (as he saw it) 'winter of imperial withdrawal' and, recalling his talks with Jean Monnet in Algiers, he knew that the 'spring of Europe could not be far behind'.

This was a period of determined planning for the reconstruction of post-war Europe. The Lend-Lease Act had come to an end with the fall of Japan, but its place had been taken in 1947 by the Marshall Plan, providing American aid towards economic recovery in Europe. In 1948, the Organisation for European Economic Cooperation (OECC) came into being to help administer the Marshall Plan. In April 1949, the signing of the North Atlantic Treaty in Washington brought NATO into being, further bringing into focus the concept of supranational cooperation, in this instance in the realms of defence.

Throughout this period, Macmillan played an active and supportive role, with Churchill, in many of the various strands of the emerging European movement. He was far more loyal and vocal in his support of Churchill's 'United States of Europe' speeches and initiatives between 1945 and 1951 than Eden, Churchill's ultimate (and soon-regretted) successor. He was a key supporter of the British Committee of the European League for Economic Cooperation (ELEC), co-founding an Eastern European group within ELEC to try to maintain economic links with Soviet Bloc-occupied countries; and, in 1950, he became one of the Conservative members attending parliamentary sessions of the Assembly of the newly created Council of Europe.

The Council of Europe was founded in May 1949 and brought into being by the Treaty of London. It was born out of the United European Movement (UEM), a pan-European organisation created two years earlier in 1947, under Churchill's leadership, to underpin the post-war reconstruction of Europe. Macmillan was a prominent enthusiast for the UEM from its outset, serving on its management committee and attending the first Congress of Europe, which met at The Hague in May 1948 with Churchill in the chair. The following year, Macmillan was a founder member of the Council of Europe, becoming equally enthusiastically involved; he was to serve as one of the six 'opposition' Conservative delegates to the Assembly, speaking regularly at the Strasbourg meetings, for the next three years.

Macmillan's experience as one of a group of members, described by one historian as the 'Tory Strasbourgers', was an important and formative one. He not only enjoyed the experience of being in Strasbourg (even when Churchill paid his presidential visits and business was done late into the night), but also gained first-hand experience of the complexities of European politics. It placed him more firmly in the public eye in the capital cities of Western Europe. In August 1949, Macmillan deputised for Churchill (after the former Prime Minister had suffered a stroke), winding up an important debate on the future position of West Germany that led to its joining the Council of Europe in 1950.

The political divisions within the Assembly were primarily between those who sought a more informal cooperation within Europe (Macmillan was firmly in this camp – 'confederation' is how he describes it often in his diaries) and those looking to undiluted political federation. Perceptively, Macmillan could already foresee the tensions that would grow within the Conservative Party, especially within what we now know as the Eurosceptic wing, who in those days feared what they saw as the threat to Britain's relationship with the Empire and the Commonwealth; it was to become a split that has divided the party ever since.

On 9 May 1950, the French Foreign Minister Robert Schuman set out his proposals at the Quai d'Orsay for pooling the coal and steel production of France and Germany, and any other Western European country that wished to join, under the control of a single, independent supranational authority. The Schuman Declaration was explicitly intended to be a first step towards political integration, an objective that Schuman believed was essential to bring West Germany into a closer alliance with the rest of Europe and one that would therefore deliver lasting peace. Macmillan thought Schuman's proposals were 'an act of high courage and imaginative statesmanship'.

When the Labour government subsequently refused to enter into dialogue over Schuman's plans ('If you open that Pandora's box, you never know what Trojan horses will jump out' was the oft-quoted reaction of the Foreign Secretary Ernest Bevin), Macmillan was outspoken in his criticism – a 'black week for Britain; for the Empire; for Europe; and for the peace of the world'. The initiative, he wrote in his diary, 'may well be a major turning-point in European history. It is certainly a turning-point in the fortunes of the Tory Party. This issue affords us the last, and perhaps only, chance of regaining the initiative.' On 22 May, he wrote to *The Times* supporting Schuman and was duly subjected to a barrage of criticism at home.

Yet for all Macmillan's 'general Europhilia', his support for the European project was far from unconditional and a good deal more nuanced than it appears at first glance. While he admired the motives and ambition of those seeking closer European integration, he was no fan of the way in which the process of government was conducted. At the Council of Europe session in August 1950, also attended by Churchill, Macmillan made the keynote speech on behalf of the Conservatives in response to the Schuman Plan. He warned his European counterparts that there remained a fundamental difference within Europe that was both:

> temperamental and intellectual … it is based on a long divergence of two states of mind and methods of organisation. The Continental tradition likes to reason *a priori* from the top downwards, from the general principle to the practical application … The Anglo-Saxons like to argue *a posteriori* from the bottom upwards, from practical experience.

In October 1951, Attlee called a general election, hoping to increase his wafer-thin majority; in the event, in spite of Labour winning the popular vote (albeit on account of unopposed returns in Northern Ireland), Churchill was returned for his third administration at the age of seventy-six. Eden became Foreign Secretary and Macmillan Minister of Housing, with the brief to build 300,000 homes. It was a brief to make or break his career. It made it: Macmillan built the houses.

Among historians of the European project, opinion is divided as to the importance of the first two years of the new Churchill government. Was this a crucial, missed early opportunity to become a member of the EEC? The more popular school of thought is that both the Labour government, pre-1951, and the Conservative government that succeeded it, did indeed miss a golden opportunity to join the negotiations and to shape the embryonic European Coal and Steel Community. The opposing view is that those like Macmillan, who had previously believed Churchill to be a steadfast supporter of the European project, were mistaken. There is no doubt that Macmillan and his allies believed Churchill to be a committed European and felt deeply let down by his behaviour in 1951 and 1952. When challenged by the junior Foreign Office minister and protégé of Eden's, Anthony Nutting, as to why he had made the various speeches that he had in support of European unity in the late 1940s, Churchill replied, 'Well, I really meant it for them and not for us.'

Macmillan and his closest ally at the Council of Europe (David Maxwell Fyfe, veteran advocate of the Nuremberg war trials and now Home Secretary) had viewed the Labour government of Attlee and Bevin as anti-European and were hoping, given Churchill's previous rhetoric, for a change of British policy. The hopes of the Conservative Europhiles were quickly dashed, however. On 28 November 1951, Eden announced in Rome that Britain would not participate in a European army, the so-called Pleven Plan, named after the French Defence minister who had originally brought forward the proposal, René Pleven. Yet in Strasbourg, Conservative delegates continued to encourage the idea. In Cabinet a few days later, Churchill supported the Eden line and made a point of asking Macmillan and Maxwell Fyfe if they were satisfied. Macmillan recorded his reply in his diary: he thought 'the present position tragic' but was forced to accept it. He feared that the position in ten years' time would very likely be worse, 'with a European Community which would dominate Europe ... If we stay out, we risk that German domination of Europe which we have fought two world wars to prevent.'

Eden was no supporter of the Council of Europe and Macmillan viewed both the Foreign Secretary and the Foreign Office as a whole as 'quite unrepentant ... they clearly mean to destroy Strasbourg'. On 13 March 1952, the Cabinet met to discuss the Council, Macmillan first having circulated a paper which he doubted anyone had read in advance. Eden was absent convalescing and sent Anthony Nutting (who was to resign from government, never to return, a few years later during the Suez Crisis) in his place. Macmillan set out his position, which was received in polite silence, with only Maxwell Fyfe offering support, while Lord Salisbury was blatantly hostile. The rest, he recorded in his diary, were 'largely ignorant'. Churchill was 'clearly uneasy [and] did nothing to help'.

Over the course of the next few days, Macmillan seriously considered resignation, the only time he was to do so over the issue of Europe in the course of his career. He was quietly furious with Churchill: 'I don't believe he realises the sense of disappointment or even anger of those whom he led in five years work in the European movement.' A divided Cabinet meant that discussions on Europe were 'very painful'; those members he viewed as 'functionaries' did not understand the issues and Churchill himself was 'puzzled and unhappy'. In the end, Macmillan stayed put; to have resigned then, he admitted many years later, would have been a 'terrible mistake' – for the party with a small majority, for the pro-European cause (there was 'no enthusiasm in the country whatsoever for Europe', he admitted) and for his own career.

Macmillan's formidable task at Housing made it difficult for him to be heard in respect of other matters of state, including Europe. In March 1953, he circulated a further paper, opposing a federal Europe as being against Britain's national interest. On 1 September 1953, he went to see Churchill to talk about the future. When Macmillan confirmed that the Foreign Office was his ambition, Churchill laughed 'and said he supposed I felt he had rather let down the European movement. But it was inevitable. We had got in too late, and things had hardened.'

When Churchill finally retired in April 1955, Eden succeeded him as Prime Minister and immediately called a general election. The Conservatives were returned with a greatly increased majority and Eden appointed Macmillan to his own former position, that of Foreign Secretary. While the two men had worked together in both government and opposition for many years, the relationship between them was cordial rather than warm, and (as David Dutton also explains) they disagreed fundamentally on Europe.

On 1 June 1955, the six Foreign Ministers of the European Coal and Steel Community (ECSC) met at Messina in Sicily, at Jean Monnet's instigation, to consider the foundation of a European common market. The ECSC had developed from Schuman's original proposal of May 1950, had been ratified at the Treaty of Paris in April 1951, and the so-called High Authority (the precursor of today's European Commission and the first supranational European institution) had assumed office in August 1952 under Monnet's presidency. The six members were France, West Germany, Italy, Belgium, the Netherlands and Luxembourg. The Belgian Foreign Minister, Paul-Henri Spaak, was chosen to chair the committee that would write the blueprint, and draft a formal treaty, for a European common market.

The timing of the Messina conference was bad for Britain: Churchill was barely out of Downing Street, and Eden and Macmillan were both new to their respective jobs. Eden had, on numerous occasions, made clear his belief that Britain could never join a European political federation of the kind proposed by Monnet; Britain's ties, he insisted, were with the United States and the Commonwealth. Not only did Britain fail to send a serious representative (only a junior observer), the subsequent approaches made by the Six were rebuffed. The Chancellor of the Exchequer, Rab Butler, described the Messina conference as 'some archaeological excavations' in an old Sicilian town, of no concern to Britain. Macmillan did not agree, but neither did he welcome the proposals wholly enthusiastically – he continued to favour confederation over federation.

At Messina, and during the Brussels negotiations afterwards, the Six wanted Britain to participate from the start. It is generally acknowledged today that a key opportunity to join and to shape the fledgling EEC was missed at this time. Macmillan's biographer, Alistair Horne, observes how Macmillan's political career was characterised by keeping a number of balls in the air, but that in the case of the founding of the EEC, 'one ball was dropped which seems not to have been immediately apparent at the time'.

On 14 December, Macmillan attended a meeting of the Western European Union in Paris. Spaak in particular was sharply critical of Britain's reaction to Messina, which the Six believed (almost certainly correctly) was an attempt to undermine the outcome of the conference. Macmillan replied sarcastically that previously Britain 'had been accused for concealing our policy till it was too late … Now they complained that we had revealed it prematurely.' He made it clear that while Britain would 'welcome and assist the plan', there was no question of joining in.

Invited to join Spaak's committee at ministerial level, the government instead sent a civil servant to follow the committee's deliberations. In November 1955, Britain withdrew from the negotiations altogether.

The negotiations post-Messina were touch and go. When Macmillan saw Spaak in Paris in early 1956, the chairman of his eponymous committee confessed that he 'took a very depressing view of Europe. France was no good; Italy hovering on the verge of Communism; Germany becomes more and more aggressive'. France, he thought, would never enter a true common market. Could not, Spaak implored Macmillan, the 'UK take the lead'?

In a Cabinet reshuffle just before Christmas 1955, Eden, unexpectedly, and much to Macmillan's annoyance, moved him to the Treasury, where he succeeded Rab Butler as Chancellor. Macmillan's biographer D. R. Thorpe describes Macmillan's reaction as 'astonished and deeply disappointed'; he was enjoying Foreign Office work and resented being moved again so quickly. Contemporary press coverage largely commented on Macmillan being too strong a Foreign Secretary for Eden, who, having held the post for so many years himself, preferred to keep a tight grip over the portfolio. On arriving at the Treasury, Macmillan confided to his diary: 'I don't feel I know what to do next – esp. in the field of overseas policy. A merely negative attitude to European cooperation (as put forward by the Messina plan and the Six powers) is not enough. We ought to try to find a constructive alternative.'

Britain was forced to decide whether to allow EEC integration to continue without check, leaving the country increasingly isolated, or, as Macmillan suggested, to find an alternative solution. The prospect of an inner European customs union with an external tariff, harmful to Commonwealth trading interests, was an unappealing one. Macmillan and Peter Thorneycroft, the President of the Board of Trade, set about looking for an alternative structure, one where tariff barriers with Europe would be largely abolished, but preferential trading for Commonwealth imports, mainly agricultural, would be maintained. After a number of attempts to solve the conundrum, they finally came up with the so-called Plan G, the forerunner of what was later to be known from 1959 as the European Free Trade Association (EFTA).

As a vehicle for delivering the plan, the Organisation for European Economic Cooperation (OEEC), created in 1948 to administer the Marshall Plan, appeared to be the most suitable. On 27 July, as the Suez Crisis engulfed the country, Macmillan and Thorneycroft put their report to the Cabinet: 'UK Initiatives in Europe: Plan G'. The proposal to abolish the high tariffs that had traditionally protected British industry against cheap imports was a potentially controversial one, and Macmillan recognised that he would have difficulty selling it to his own backbenchers and even to some of his Cabinet colleagues. In fact, even the ministers within his own department were divided on its merits.

The continuing subsidies to support Commonwealth food imports and some other products crucial to Commonwealth trade, while a sine qua non for his Cabinet colleagues, were never likely to be accepted by the Six – and so it proved, in spite of a brief wobble for the Spaak negotiations in October. Nevertheless, Macmillan formally presented the plan to a meeting of

Commonwealth finance ministers at the Washington embassy in September and, reporting to the Cabinet on his return, he again stressed that Commonwealth 'preference' must be preserved. He hoped that Plan G would provide the necessary economic link between the inner 'Six' and the outer 'Seven' (Austria, Britain, Denmark, Norway, Portugal, Sweden and Switzerland), but without the need for any political commitment. Negotiations were to continue for two years.

The problem for Macmillan and Plan G enthusiasts was that the world at the time was fully focused on the Suez Crisis. At the Commonwealth ministers' meeting, in Cabinet, at the Conservative Party conference and even in the House of Commons, Macmillan noted 'a certain unreality about the discussions' as everyone found it 'difficult to deal with more than one great issue at a time'. In spite of this, many governments in Europe, including the French, were broadly supportive, but negotiations were slowed by the refusal to take any final decision on Britain's plan until the Treaty of Rome had been ratified.

In the wake of Suez, and suffering from poor health, Eden resigned on 9 January 1957 and Macmillan became Prime Minister. On 25 March 1957, while Macmillan was meeting with Eisenhower in Bermuda, the 'Six' signed the Treaty of Rome that would bring the EEC into being on 1 January 1958. In Alistair Horne's words again, 'the historic signature seems to have passed almost unnoticed by Macmillan'. There is no mention of it in his diary for that day, and only a passing reference to EFTA for that week.

De Gaulle's return to power in May 1958, following a revolt

in Algeria and the fall of the Fourth Republic, was to mark the beginning of the end for Plan G. The two leaders initially exchanged warm personal messages and Macmillan visited Paris at the end of June. De Gaulle's manner was 'calm, affable and rather paternal … but underneath this new exterior, I should judge that he is just as obstinate as ever'. Macmillan recalled from their wartime friendship de Gaulle's fierce nationalism and deep distrust of both Britain and the United States. So it was to prove. The Algerian crisis, which had brought him to power, and local French constitutional politics, were now de Gaulle's priorities. Europe in general, and Plan G in particular, were some way down his list.

It was clear that de Gaulle and Konrad Adenauer were to be the two dominant leaders in Europe. Adenauer had been Chancellor of West Germany since 1949, and Macmillan recognised that as a strong supporter of European integration he was crucial to the negotiations. Macmillan sought to use Adenauer as a means of getting to de Gaulle: 'No British government,' he warned Adenauer, 'could continue to take part in the military defence of a continent which had declared economic war upon her. The United Kingdom would become isolationist.'

However, the tactic failed. De Gaulle convinced the German leader that Britain should not be admitted to the EEC, and nor should the Six join in plans for a wider free trade area. Macmillan made one last appeal to de Gaulle: part threat ('how can we prevent political antagonisms as well as economic rivalries from springing up?') and part appeal to 'our old friendship'. However, on 14 November, de Gaulle vetoed outright the concept of the Six joining the EFTA and a few days later he was elected President of France. For Macmillan, it was a bitter blow, an indicator and precursor of further blows to come.

On 1 January 1960, Sir Frank Lee became Joint Permanent Secretary to the Treasury, in succession to the former Washington ambassador Sir Roger Makins, whose wartime distrust of de Gaulle had always coloured his view of Europe. Lee, on the other hand, was an 'impassioned advocate of European integration' and his appointment, more than any other contemporary event, forced a change of policy and direction in respect of Britain's and Macmillan's relationship with Europe. The historian Jacqueline Tratt states that Lee's memorandum 'The Six and the Seven' 'stands out as the definitive document that was to set Britain on a new course, not only in terms of trade but also in terms of Britain's political role and outlook'.

In July 1960, Macmillan summed up in his diary the growing danger, as he saw it, of Britain remaining outside the EEC:

> Shall we be caught between a hostile (or at least less and less friendly) America and a boastful, powerful 'Empire of Charlemagne'– now under French but later bound to come under German control. Is this the real reason for 'joining' the Common Market (if we are acceptable) and for abandoning (a) the Seven (b) British agriculture (c) the Commonwealth? It's a grim choice.

In July 1961, the Cabinet decided to apply to join the EEC, a momentous decision and one of Macmillan's most important initiatives that was to define the remaining years of his premiership. The task was monumental. In the first place, Macmillan would have to juggle the competing concerns of the Americans (with whom he had enjoyed a strong relationship, never more so than now with President Kennedy), the Commonwealth and the other members of the so-called Seven outer states of EFTA. On 31 July, Macmillan told the House of Commons that Britain would join the EEC only if satisfactory arrangements could be made for the Commonwealth, EFTA and British agriculture; these were indeed the key issues that were to dominate the negotiations.

Macmillan hoped that Britain could provide a sturdy bridge between mainland Europe and America. His aim, he recorded in a Cabinet paper, 'The Grand Design', was to 'call attention to the need to organise the great forces of the Free World – USA, Britain and Europe – economically, politically and militarily in a coherent effort to withstand the Communist tide all over the world.'

Formal negotiations between Britain and the Six began, symbolically, initially in Paris and then in Brussels, in October 1961. Macmillan knew that the French attitude would be crucial. In advance of the talks, he acknowledged that de Gaulle's prior agreement to the objectives of the negotiations was vital. 'This will have to be done,' pondered Macmillan, 'but HOW I am not sure.' He was correct that de Gaulle saw things very differently: he wanted a Europe that would be a third important world power, led of course by France and he did not trust Britain's intentions in respect of the United States or the Commonwealth.

Edward Heath, the deputy Foreign Secretary, took the political lead in the negotiations, while, as a sop to de Gaulle, Britain's chief civil service negotiator was Sir Pierson Dixon, a former member of Macmillan's staff in Algiers, and now ambassador in Paris. The French, however, were deeply distrustful and at the Birch Grove meeting the following month (called at de Gaulle's suggestion), the French President skilfully batted away all Macmillan's efforts to open more positive discussions. De Gaulle was only too happy to drag his feet, refusing to weaken his negotiating position by giving any indication whatsoever that he might be favourable to Britain's application.

While Heath and Macmillan were publicly upbeat when reporting on the progress of negotiations, it soon became clear that the negotiators of the Six were in no mood to make significant concessions. As Macmillan had predicted, future trading arrangements with the Commonwealth proved to be a key stumbling block. After the Birch Grove meeting of November 1961, de Gaulle's domestic standing was greatly strengthened the following year when his supporters won a majority in the French National Assembly. In addition, de Gaulle's call for the French President to be elected by direct popular vote, rather than via an electoral college, was backed by voters in a national referendum.

In December 1962, in the wake of the Cuban Missile Crisis and prior to flying to Nassau to see President Kennedy, Macmillan visited de Gaulle at Rambouillet, the chateau on the outskirts of Paris traditionally used by French Presidents as their second residence. As so often, de Gaulle had felt snubbed by what he perceived as the closeness of British–US negotiations, to France's exclusion – in particular in respect of an independent nuclear deterrent. In defence matters, de Gaulle told Macmillan at Rambouillet, Britain was not 'truly European'; he was equally aggravated by his belief that the British nuclear force was not 'purely British', but was in fact 'closely linked to the United States'.

In spite of a morning's shooting (de Gaulle ostentatiously refused to join in, preferring to sit behind Macmillan gleefully drawing attention to his missed shots), the atmosphere was more formal and businesslike than it had been at Birch Grove. Whether conversing while walking in the woods, or meeting more formally in the chateau, it was clear to the British delegation that the talks were not going well. On the second morning, in the full plenary session with both delegations, de Gaulle at last revealed his hand. In a long, rambling speech, he made it clear that while he might one day welcome Britain into the EEC, he did not believe the time was yet right. Macmillan was 'shocked and dismayed'.

A few days later de Gaulle told a meeting of his Council of Ministers that he preferred Macmillan's Britain to that of the Labour Party, and would like to help him remain in power. 'But what could I do?' he enquired disparagingly, 'except sing to him Edith Piaf's song *Ne pleurez pas, Milord*'. As if to compound Macmillan's humiliation, the comment was widely leaked to the press.

On 14 January 1963, just as the Brussels negotiations were reconvening post-Christmas, de Gaulle called a press conference at the Élysée Palace attended by 800 assorted journalists, foreign diplomats, French politicians and civil servants. Britain, he said, was 'insular, she is maritime, she is linked through her exchanges, her markets, her supply lines to the most diverse and often the distant countries; she pursues essentially industrial and commercial activities, and only slightly agricultural ones'. Britain had failed to put Europe first, continuing to place Commonwealth and US interests above European ones.

De Gaulle's veto came as a terrible blow to Macmillan, arguably one from which his premiership never recovered. 'All our policies at home and abroad are in ruins,' he recorded in his diary; it was 'a political, psychological and physical blow' from which he never recovered. A place at the top table in Europe was to have been 'Macmillan's ace', writes D. R. Thorpe, 'and de Gaulle trumped it'. From the time of Messina onwards, Macmillan had enjoyed a position of political power as Eden's Foreign Secretary, then Chancellor of the Exchequer and finally as Prime Minister himself. He must therefore, concludes Thorpe, 'take his portion of the blame for the lack of clarity and commitment in the British approach to European membership'.

CHAPTER 5

ALEC DOUGLAS-HOME

ANDREW HOLT

'It occurs to me that the bachelor surrenders some of his sovereignty on marriage; but, by and large, marriage benefits the human race.'

LORD HOME IN HOUSE OF LORDS DEBATE ON JOINING THE EUROPEAN COMMUNITY, 1961

Sir Alec Douglas-Home was present at some of the defining moments in Britain's relationship with Europe in the twentieth century. Having entered the House of Commons after the 1931 general election, Lord Dunglass – the courtesy title by which Douglas-Home was then known – was appointed parliamentary private secretary to the Chancellor of the Exchequer, Neville Chamberlain, in February 1936. He remained with Chamberlain when the Chancellor succeeded Stanley Baldwin as Prime Minister the following year and accompanied him to his final meeting with Adolf Hitler at Munich in September

1938. Sitting outside the conference room, Douglas-Home conversed with the head of the German Armed Forces High Command, and 'watched as [Hermann] Göring changed his uniform three times during the day' and 'Mussolini strutted about with his chin in the air'.

Douglas-Home had inherited his father's earldom and risen to the post of Foreign Secretary by the time Harold Macmillan sought to take Britain into the European Economic Community (EEC). Douglas-Home's appointment was controversial, not least because of his presence in the upper house, and it was left to Edward Heath, his deputy, to speak on foreign affairs in the House of Commons. It was Heath who was charged with leading the EEC negotiations. Douglas-Home had no objection to this arrangement, however, and supported Heath's efforts when meeting with European leaders. Douglas-Home was in a similar position after returning to the Foreign Office in 1970 at the beginning of Heath's premiership. While he took his place next to the Prime Minister at the January 1972 Treaty of Accession signing ceremony, Anthony Barber (briefly) and Geoffrey Rippon had taken the lead on EEC matters. Douglas-Home's own short premiership was less eventful where European developments were concerned. The circumstances did not lend themselves to progress. When he succeeded Macmillan in October 1963 – renouncing his peerage in the process – Britain's first EEC application had been blocked by French President Charles de Gaulle and a general election was due within a year.

Douglas-Home was supportive of British membership of the common market. As one of his early biographers John Dickie wrote, 'Lord Home certainly did not demonstrate the crusading enthusiasm that Edward Heath showed in Brussels. But he had strong convictions that Britain should not exclude herself from the European movement'. Douglas-Home's own writing provides limited insight into his views on European integration. His 1976 autobiography reveals little, while *Letters to a Grandson* highlights his stronger interest in the Cold War and related issues.

Douglas-Home did, however, concisely outline his views in August 1961, when moving a House of Lords motion to open EEC membership negotiations. He based his support for entry on the political assumption that Britain wished to retain global political influence and remain a leading partner in the Commonwealth. His expertise in foreign and colonial affairs was much greater than his knowledge of economics, but he did see joining the common market as a way of improving living standards. Regarding sovereignty Douglas-Home was pragmatic. He argued that 'when we are considering this question of sovereignty it is really a matter of balance of advantage. We should not make sovereignty into a shibboleth. It occurs to me,' he went on, 'that the bachelor surrenders some of his sovereignty on marriage; but, by and large marriage benefits the human race.'

Douglas-Home became Prime Minister just months after French President Charles de Gaulle had vetoed Britain's application to join the common market. Nothing had changed by October 1964. The Conservative election manifesto stated that, 'Entry into the European Economic Community is not open to us in existing circumstances, and no question of fresh negotiations can arise at present.'

That was not because Douglas-Home had cooled on the principle of joining the common market. The arguments he expressed in the summer of 1961 still stood and other European leaders remained supportive of Britain's membership. There was growing concern within the Foreign Office as to what might await Britain if the country remained outside. Con O'Neill, the British ambassador to the EEC, warned Foreign Secretary Rab Butler that it was difficult to see an effective future for the UK unless a 'satisfactory relationship' with the six EEC members was established, especially when they were on good terms with the United States. 'Without a satisfactory link between this country and the European Communities, within an Atlantic framework, we will suffer a relative, perhaps rather rapid, decline towards isolation and reduced influence.'

Gaston Defferre, a potential Socialist candidate for the French presidency, told Douglas-Home in April 1964 that he hoped Britain would join the common market, and that the question could be reconsidered under a new French government. But Douglas-Home thought nothing could be done while de Gaulle was in power. In a handwritten note on a dispatch from Britain's ambassador to France, which stated that 'We could hope to lead Europe, and must try to join it'. Douglas-Home wrote 'when the General goes we should try & lead Europe'.

Britain's failure to join the EEC also influenced Douglas-Home's attitude to cooperation with European allies on defence. The multilateral force (MLF) was to be a nuclear-armed naval fleet manned by mixed crews from NATO countries. It was intended primarily to give West Germany a say in nuclear matters and reduce the likelihood that the Germans might be tempted to develop their own weapons. The only other country to show an interest was Italy, whose Prime Minister told Douglas-Home that 'the MLF gave the Italians and Germans the opportunity to play their rightful role in the world'. In January 1964, the Italian Foreign Minister insinuated privately that British support for the MLF was necessary for the Italians to back her EEC ambitions.

British reactions veered between indifference and hostility. The Minister of Defence, Peter Thorneycroft, was in the latter camp. Militarily, the scheme was of dubious utility. Field Marshal Bernard Montgomery called mixed-manning 'utter and complete poppycock'. It was expensive, too, with the projected cost to Britain of £150 million over ten years the equivalent of two aircraft carriers or three Polaris submarines. The MLF antagonised the Soviet Union, which had particular concerns that nuclear weapons assigned to the force could at some point in the future be deployed independently of the United States. When the MLF looked increasingly likely to come into force whatever, he pointed out the 'cogent argument' that Britain should join the MLF to keep her finger on the trigger whatever the US may decide in the future.

On the other hand, Macmillan had signed up to the MLF and the Americans were exerting significant pressure. The Foreign Office highlighted the European dimension of the force. Butler argued that the failure to enter the EEC had damaged British influence in Europe and the US. He feared that to stay out of the MLF would be to repeat the mistake. The indications were that the MLF would go ahead without Britain and could become the forum for wider cooperation in which Britain would have little influence. Ambassador to France Sir Pierson Dixon meanwhile saw the MLF as a possible way to distract the Six from pressing ahead with political union without Britain. Douglas-Home eventually came down on the side of joining the MLF for political reasons, though he did so without any great belief in the project. As with European political integration, he sought to delay any major public commitment until after the election.

Douglas-Home narrowly lost the October 1964 general election. When the party returned to government in 1970 with Ted Heath as Prime Minister, Douglas-Home became Foreign Secretary once again. Douglas-Home's role in the European accession negotiations was limited but his practicality complemented Heath's gusto and his backing for membership carried weight with the right of the Conservative Party.

Lacking the passion and enthusiasm of Ted Heath, Douglas-Home's pro-Europeanism was pragmatic. 'If, as is certain, power is to lie in Europe', he told the House of Lords in August 1961, 'then I think it is there that Britain ought to be.' While he remained committed to the Commonwealth, he acknowledged that 'the Commonwealth is not a centre of power'. Douglas-Home was also mindful of Britain's diminished status, but he had no wish to give up on a world role. He thought that British membership of the EEC, NATO and the Commonwealth gave her a unique opportunity to exert influence in the world.

CHAPTER 6

HAROLD WILSON

ANDREW ADONIS

'But whatever the economic arguments ... the government's purpose derives, above all, from our recognition that Europe is now faced with the opportunity of a great move forward in political unity and that we can, and indeed must, play our full part in it.'

HAROLD WILSON PROPOSING BRITAIN'S SECOND APPLICATION TO JOIN THE EUROPEAN COMMUNITY IN THE HOUSE OF COMMONS, 1967

Harold Wilson performed more somersaults on Europe than an Olympic gymnast. But he ended up with gold. By the time he had finished his twelve-year performance, from becoming Labour leader in 1963 to the 'common market' referendum of 1975, he had achieved a triumph remarkable in its own right – a two-to-one popular majority for membership – and one utterly amazing in light of David Cameron's failure in 2016. The fact that a re-run did not take place for forty-one years, and that the re-run itself took the form of Cameron attempting to mimic Wilson, raises his podium higher still.

So how did he pull it off?

Wilson was good at winning elections; better numerically than any of his post-war predecessors and successors bar none. He fought five elections and won four, albeit one (February 1974) as the largest party in a hung parliament. He was tactically agile and at his best almost faultless. 'If you cannot ride three horses at the same time, you should not be in the circus,' was his mantra. With a creed of fairly unthreatening, provincial, classless, middle-of-the-road, painless social democratic managerialism, Wilson assembled a Labour coalition rivalled by only two other leaders in Labour's entire history: Attlee and Blair. But Wilson held his coalition together longer than either of them, winning elections over a ten-year period (1964 to 1974) – they managed only five and eight years respectively – and he expanded it wider, into Tory heartlands, to win the 1975 referendum as his concluding act.

Wilson was as persuasive and unthreatening in personality as in policy, which was integral to his appeal. (As Jonathan Freedland puts it so well: 'People don't believe in ideas, they believe in people who believe in ideas.') Bernard Donoughue, Wilson's Downing Street policy director in his last government, gives this insightful portrait:

> Of medium height, always smartly dressed, his face was soft, nothing sharp or aggressive about him. He avoided confrontations, leaving that to his hard men, Joe Haines and Marcia

> Falkender [*sic*]. His accent was softly north country, more so when addressing trade unionists or party rank and file. With his good manners and quiet humour, he always made people feel at ease, whatever their party, race or gender.

Or class, one might add – he was a favourite of the Queen. He also had a great line in props: pipe, Gannex mac and Paddy the Labrador are up there with Churchill's cigars and bow ties, and a cut or two above Blair's jeans and guitar.

Wilson had few bitter enemies. Roy Jenkins, who resigned as Labour deputy leader in 1972 over Wilson's decision to back a European referendum and clashed with him repeatedly over his 'tergiversations' on Europe (Jenkins's word, which shows how little he possessed of Wilson's populist touch), never disliked him personally. They worked closely in government before and after. A hard biographical taskmaster, Jenkins wrote a sympathetic appreciation of his former sparring partner for the *Dictionary of National Biography* shortly before his death in 2003. 'He was a very considerable servant of the state. He kept the train of government on the rails over difficult stretches of country,' was Jenkins's verdict. Tony Benn, a former protégé who broke with Wilson to lead the anti-Europe referendum campaign as part of his dash to the left, noted ruefully in his diary the day after defeat: 'He's the cleverest political leader we have had for a long time.'

Personal emollience, tactical brilliance, underlying public interest: this combination animated Wilson's European policy throughout his thirteen years as Labour leader, and explain his ultimate triumph in keeping Britain in Europe.

Wilson was 'for' but not 'of' Europe, temperamentally and philosophically. He spoke no European languages (but then neither did Heath nor even Jenkins until he worked on his French in order to become President of the European Commission in 1977). As an Oxford undergraduate, Wilson never travelled abroad in the 1930s; his college, Jesus, was home to many Welsh students, not Adam von Trott and the international clientele of the Balliol College of Heath, Jenkins and Healey.

After Oxford, Wilson was drafted as a wartime civil servant working on statistics and economics for Lord Beveridge, among others. He never saw overseas or military service, which perhaps not coincidentally gave him more in common with Margaret Thatcher (at Somerville College in the mid-1940s) than his male contemporaries. After he married Mary, later a poet admired by Poet Laureate John Betjeman, they didn't go to the Continent on holiday, as the Jenkins family did religiously. Nor was there much interest in European art and culture, in the manner of Heath playing the first of Johann Sebastian Bach's forty-eight preludes and fugues on his grand piano in No. 10 after the Commons vote in favour of accession to the European Community on 28 October 1971, when Wilson voted against.

Jenkins observed, 'There was a deep-rooted provincialism about Wilson which persisted throughout his national political career, and indeed in many ways enhanced it, the Scilly Islands sometimes seeming the limit of his global reach.' Social disdain tinged with political respect.

However, Wilson wasn't just English. He also identified strongly with the 'white Commonwealth,' as did so many of the twentieth-century English with relatives in Australia, Canada and New Zealand. One of Wilson's few long foreign excursions was six months in Australia at the age of ten to visit his grandfather. When Prime Minister, he claimed to have forty-three close relations in the Antipodes of Australia, animating his 'fight' for 'kith and kin' in opposition to Heath 'selling out' the Commonwealth on beef, lamb, butter and cheese – literally bread and butter politics, at which Wilson excelled.

Surveying Wilson's pronouncements across his political career from becoming MP for Ormskirk in 1945 until resignation in April 1976, his position on Europe is strikingly mainstream at every stage. He was mainstream in opposing the creation and early British membership of the European institutions in the 1940s and 1950s; then mainstream again in moving gradually to support membership of the European Community in the 1960s and '70s. However, it wasn't a smooth trajectory. There were calculated lurches and the lurches, characteristic of Wilson operating on a controversial issue, may account for his ultimate success.

Wilson's two most important lurches were his strongly pro-European pitches at two key moments of power: the 1967 application to join the European Community and the 1974–75 renegotiation of membership and recommendation in favour of staying in the European Community in the subsequent June 1975 referendum. However, of tactical significance were his two lurches in the other direction at key moments of vulnerability: in the early 1960s, when vying for the Labour leadership, and in the early 1970s, when scheming to retain it after losing the 1970 election.

There are crucial differences betwen these two anti-European phases. In 1962 and '63 Wilson, like Gaitskell whom he was seeking to replace, would have been content, in the short term at least, to stay outside the European Community, although both men recognised Macmillan's economic and strategic arguments for membership. By contrast, in the early 1970s, Wilson's support for joining the EC was obviously a matter of historical record, and only shameless, if adroit, manoeuvring enabled him to pivot from proposing to join in 1967, to voting against Heath's accession agreement in 1971, to leading a government committed to staying barely two years later.

When Wilson decided to make the second application in 1967, Hugh Cudlipp, editor of the pro-European *Daily Mirror*, noted caustically that his 'discovery' of Europe was a gigantic attempt 'to distract attention from Rhodesia and the economic mess at home', in light of the failed negotiations with Ian Smith over Rhodesian independence and the likely devaluation of sterling. However, more significant is what Rhodesia and devaluation said about British weakness: an ex-colonial power unable to force a white supremacist to share power with the black majority in a small British colony in southern Africa; and an economy so weak that it could not even defend an exchange rate with the dollar which had been proclaimed a matter of critical national interest. Wilson, a realist, grasped both points and the imperative therefore for strong European engagement, however tactical his short-term manoeuvring.

Wilson's preparatory tour of European capitals in 1966–67, with his pro-European (if habitually drunk) Foreign Secretary

George Brown, made him almost evangelically pro-European, until de Gaulle put the final kibosh on the British application nine days after devaluation in November 1967. This double humiliation made the argument for redoubling efforts to get into Europe all the greater in Wilson's mind, which is why he was preparing, in the event of the expected Labour victory in the 1970 election, to appoint his strongly pro-European Chancellor Roy Jenkins to the Foreign Office to make a third application, now that de Gaulle had retired. Had Wilson won in 1970, Britain would almost certainly have joined the European Community on very similar timescale and terms to those followed by Heath.

When the electorate unexpectedly put Heath in power in 1970, James Callaghan played a populist anti-European card in a bid to rally Labour's trade union centre ground against a greatly weakened Wilson. His big move was his 'language of Chaucer' speech in Southampton in May 1971. Seizing on President Pompidou's recent remark that French was the language of the 'new Europe', the bluff Callaghan declared a mission to save 'the language of Chaucer, Shakespeare and Milton'. He cited dubious statistics supplied by his economist son-in-law Peter Jay, later his ambassador to Washington, claiming that trade with developing countries, many of them in the Commonwealth, was greater than with the common market countries. Callaghan went into full naval 'boyhood of Rayleigh' mode on Britain continuing to look 'towards the open sea and the world beyond'. As for a French-led Europe, 'I will say it in French to prevent any misunderstanding: "Non, merci beaucoup."'

Tony Benn and the Labour left were also turning against Europe, so Callaghan represented a potentially lethal threat to Wilson. Jenkins offered Wilson a deal: if he resisted Callaghan, Jenkins's pro-European followers would support Wilson against any leadership challenge. But Wilson knew the Labour Party better than that. As Jenkins's lieutenant Bill Rodgers put it honestly: 'If Wilson loses his support on the left he won't have any at all, and we'll cut his bloody throat!' Wilson quickly shifted towards Callaghan, pronouncing the 'Tory terms' for accession unacceptable.

Further latching onto Benn's idea of a referendum on continued membership – which caused Jenkins's resignation, by now welcome as Wilson sought to insulate himself from the pro-European 'Jenkinsites' – he kicked Europe into touch for the forthcoming election. Labour would seek to 'renegotiate' the terms of membership and then put those terms to the people. This avoided any firm 1974 manifesto commitment one way or the other on membership of the European Community, quietening the internal argument within the party, while giving Wilson, as conductor of any post-election renegotiation, maximum flexibility.

For his next trick, when he unexpectedly (except perhaps to himself) returned to power in Heath's snap February 1974 election, Wilson produced the ace of spades. He appointed Callaghan Foreign Secretary and put him in charge of the promised renegotiation.

By now Britain had been in the EU for more than a year, uneventfully so far as relations with the EEC were concerned. Ever the realist, Callaghan was now as anxious as Wilson for a resolution that kept Britain in Europe, paving the way for him to become Wilson's successor with support of a unified Labour right wing. The 'language of Chaucer' became the language of barter, of which Callaghan was master. The new Chancellor of Germany, Helmut Schmidt, and President of France Giscard d'Estaing, both Anglophiles and English speakers, and desperate to avoid the collapse of the EEC in the midst of the 'oil shock' economic turbulence of the mid-1970s, obliged with the deals that Wilson and Callaghan sought on better access and lower consumer prices for Commonwealth meat, cheese and butter. This enabled them to proclaim a successful renegotiation. More importantly to Wilson the campaigner, it gave a strong line on cheaper food in the shops, which is why he put Commonwealth agricultural products, not arcane treaty changes or even the British contribution to the EU budget, at the centre of the renegotiation.

Not that he did much campaigning himself until the end. Wilson rightly judged that with Heath, Jenkins, William Whitelaw and Jeremy Thorpe leading the 'Yes to Europe' campaign, and the new Tory leader Margaret Thatcher dragooned into support of 'Yes', while the increasingly swivel-eyed and extremist Tony Benn and Enoch Powell led the 'No' campaign, he just needed to let the two sides slog it out and then come in prime ministerially. It worked.

Three further points matter to what happened thereafter. First, Wilson's renegotiation produced no treaty change, but nor was it a sham or a fig leaf, the folklore which David Cameron inhaled to his cost in 2015 and '16, when he thought he was pulling off a Wilson repeat. Wilson's strategy wasn't to get better answers to the theoretical questions about supranationalism and sovereignty, but to get better access to the EEC market for Commonwealth agricultural products and lower food prices in British supermarkets. This was all that mattered to him to win the referendum.

Second, it is wrong to say that the 1975 referendum was just about a common market, not a European political project. The question on the ballot paper was: 'Do you think the United Kingdom should stay in the European Community (Common Market)?' With typical Wilson finesse, this elided 'common market' and 'political union' into one concept, which is how it was seen at the time, with different emphasis depending upon who was speaking to whom about what.

However, it is the third point which is perhaps most significant; there is a large 'dog that didn't bark'. Immigration barely featured in the 1975 referendum campaign or indeed in the entire controversy about British membership of Europe in the 1970s. Why? Partly because the 'Europe of the Nine' – unlike today's 'Europe of the Twenty-Eight' – did not herald mass immigration. But, just as important, because there was, by the mid-1970s, little net immigration from the black Commonwealth, which might have confused the issue, as it did in 2016.

And why was that? Because by 1975, black immigration into Britain had been practically halted – by none other than Harold Wilson, following Enoch Powell's 1968 'rivers of blood' speech. Wilson had long before recognised the political toxicity of immigration and shut it down.

CHAPTER 7

EDWARD HEATH

MICHAEL McMANUS

There was a deep-seated belief that, if the rest of Europe could solve its problems on its own, it would no longer be likely to interfere with us in Britain. Alas, this proved to be illusory.'

EDWARD HEATH, C. 1990

Memories of the perpetually dyspeptic-looking countenance of the senescent Sir Edward Heath help to explain why negative perceptions of him remain stubbornly in place. What he always regarded as his greatest achievement – UK membership of the European Union – became an increasingly poisoned chalice, as his party slowly lost faith in Europe. To a younger generation within his own party – the party he had joined in the 1930s and never deserted until his death in 2005 – he seemed like an angry old dinosaur.

Heath's views originated not only in the scarred, burning

battlefields of war during the mainland campaign of 1944–45, but years earlier, during the remarkable experiences he had before the Second World War had broken out. He had witnessed at first hand one of the Nuremberg rallies; visited Spain at the height of its bitter Civil War; and then campaigned against the pro-appeasement Conservative candidate in the Oxford by-election of 1938.

Heath spent much of the summer of 1937 in Germany and Austria, including a particularly agreeable time as the guest of a retired professor of English, close to the Bavarian Alps. While there, he received an unexpected invitation to join a British delegation at a Nuremberg rally. In his 1977 memoir, *Travels*, Heath recalled those formative experiences:

> Professor Winckler and I talked continuously about the Nazi Party philosophy and Hitler's intentions during our long walks through the forests or when we were climbing the mountains. Neither of us had any doubt about the nature of the regime and its lack of freedom. What we perhaps did not realise was the extent to which it was already militarily committed to aggression in Europe. That was soon to become evident at Nuremberg … All the voices protesting Germany's innocence of any ill intent were stilled in my mind as I watched this demonstration of what could only be aggressive power … The finale of the Rally was a party at which Himmler was to be the host … I remember him for his soft, wet, flabby handshake. Goebbels was there, his pinched face white and sweating – evil personified.

Heath returned home from Nuremberg a convinced anti-appeaser and his experiences in Spain the following summer served only to harden his view. Writing in his autobiography, *The Course of My Life*:

> My sympathies were firmly with the elected government of the Spanish Republic simply because it was not a dictatorship, although it was somewhat to the left and was supported by the Soviet Union. Instructions in our rooms told us to go down to the basement in the event of an air-raid alarm. It was just as well that we did not heed those instructions, opting instead for the excitement of watching the bombers flying past. During one raid, a bomb went straight down the hotel lift shaft, killing all those who had rushed down to the basement shelter. A few days later, we set out to drive south from Barcelona to Tarragona and, when we were nearly halfway there, a single aeroplane flying low along the road spotted our procession of cars and machine-gunned us. His aim was poor and we were able to stop the cars, dive into the ditch alongside the road and crawl along it away from our vehicles.

When Sandy Lindsay, the master of Heath's college, Balliol, ran as an independent, anti-appeasement candidate against Tory Quentin Hogg in Oxford's so-called Munich by-election, during the autumn term of 1938, Heath actively supported him. For a young man who already harboured serious political ambitions, this was a courageous and risky move. Lindsay did not win, but he gave Hogg a genuine fright and the political authority of Neville Chamberlain was arguably never fully restored. After completing his studies in the summer of 1939, Heath went on another European holiday, this time with his lifelong best friend Madron Seligman. He found the atmosphere much changed:

> When we arrived in Berlin, we looked at the grotesque new Chancellery and then went for a full briefing from Anthony Mann, the *Daily Telegraph* correspondent there, whom I knew from Balliol days. His warnings had filled us thoroughly with foreboding by the time we caught the night train to Danzig. The atmosphere was very tense, and both Madron and I were acutely aware of how the attitude towards the British had changed among the German population. Then we decided to go by boat up-river to Warsaw. We reported to the British embassy, where the ambassador and his staff were horrified to see us. Having heard their forecast, we decided to start on the long hitch-hike back home.
>
> We saw massive German forces in tanks and trucks moving towards the Polish border, a far more threatening sight than the comparatively impotent-looking Polish troops crawling with a sense of resignation rather than fervour to the opposite side of the same frontier. Once we reached the border, we walked across the bridge over the river to safety in France. Late that night, we arrived to find a blackout and spent the night in a small hotel. The next day, we reported to the British embassy. 'Unless you get out now,' was the simple advice, 'you will never get out at all'. So full was the cross-Channel boat that, as it pulled away from the quay, it seemed about

> to capsize, taking all those waving goodbye down with it. My parents met me at Dover a week before Poland was invaded. It had not been possible for me to get in touch with them while we were away. They must have had some anxious moments, but they never mentioned them, and never complained. We had cut things pretty fine.

When war came, Heath took a leading role both in the air defence of Liverpool and the ground campaign to drive the German Army out of France and the Low Countries. What he saw during that campaign persuaded him of the senselessness of 'all-out war' and the particular futility of war between peoples who have so much in common. He witnessed at first hand the sudden, violent deaths of comrades, the shattering effect of the conflict on the lives of innocent people – and the physical destruction of much-needed homes, factories and cultural centres. In Northern Germany, ever the music lover, he was especially affected by the sight of a burned-out opera house.

Having had the proverbial 'good war', Heath, in 1950, won the suburban, Labour-held seat of Bexley with a wafer-thin majority of 133 votes. In over fifty years he never lost that seat. By the time Heath arrived in Parliament, the Conservatives were already, along with Churchill's old party the Liberals, reinventing themselves as strongly pro-European. So they remained, from the late 1940s until 1988, when Margaret Thatcher delivered her Bruges speech.

So much for the European experiences that made Heath what he was. How did he conduct his European policy in government?

For the principal accusation made against him in his latter years was that he deliberately concealed the true nature of the 'ever-closer union' aspiration of the Treaty of Rome.

The record shows that Heath, on one or possibly two occasions, chose his words ill-advisedly and may have implied that political union was not on the cards. In contrast, there are literally hundreds of speeches, articles and press releases from him, ranging across half a century of political activity from the 1950s, in which he candidly and enthusiastically spoke of the benefits (as he saw them) of political, as well as economic, unity among the peoples of Europe (or, more usually, Western Europe).

In his maiden speech in the Commons, Heath urged Attlee's government to participate in the discussions that duly led to the European Coal and Steel Community in 1951 and the Treaty of Rome in 1957. In June 1950, he criticised the Chancellor, Stafford Cripps, for always assuming the worst:

> He spoke of the high authority, suggesting that we should have no say in arranging the power of the high authority. Surely, that would not be the case. He said we should be taking a risk with the whole of our economy. We on this side of the House feel that, by standing aside from the discussions, we may be taking a very great risk with our economy in the coming years – a very great risk indeed.

Twenty-seven years later, Heath wrote in *Travels*: 'This opportunity was rejected and many of us have bitterly regretted it ever since. It cost us twenty years' delay in joining with our friends and allies in the creation of the new Europe.'

In 1956, as Chief Whip, Heath consolidated his parliamentary reputation when he held the Conservative Party together during the Suez Crisis – leaving him with a crisis of conscience that he never wholly resolved – and then deftly managed the transition from one of his mentors, Anthony Eden, to another, Harold Macmillan. Both men had been great supporters of his, as Churchill too had been – and, to some degree, all three shared his views on Europe. As Lord Privy Seal and deputy to Foreign Secretary Alec Douglas-Home between 1960 and 1963, Heath painstakingly negotiated UK accession into the EEC, only for it to be vetoed by de Gaulle. He made no attempt to conceal the potential long-term significance of what he was trying to achieve, telling the House of Commons in May 1961:

> Above all, I think that the technical and commercial matters I have mentioned must be set among the great political issues I have described. They must be set in the context of the unity of Europe and the contribution they can make towards the freedom of Europe, on the unity and freedom of which peace depends.

When the negotiations hit troubled waters in early 1962, he circulated a confidential briefing note to senior ministerial colleagues, which shows how much – or perhaps how little – has changed across over half a century:

> On the continent of Europe support for the idea of European integration comes from all sections of political opinion – except the two extremes. In several countries it has been the principal bond between the parties of the centre: and it has been a sufficiently effective bond to ensure that the great divide in politics has come not down the middle, but on either side of the centre … There are widespread misconceptions on the political obligations which we would have to accept if we join the EEC. Many people suppose that we should be entering a federal super state in which our national sovereignty would be swallowed up and which would result even in the disappearance of the British monarchy. These misconceptions thrive because of uncertainty as to the exact political content of the European communities … The Treaty of Rome has no political provisions, though an eventual political objective is implicit.

At the party conference in October 1962, Heath gave one of his best ever speeches to the party faithful, focusing on the by-now foundering accession negotiation:

> We have seen two great groups develop since the end of the last war – the United States, the Soviet Union. Now a third group, of the countries of Europe, is growing stronger – economically stronger, and with that a political cohesion developing … What is our attitude? It is that we welcome these developments in Europe. We welcome the abolition of old rivalries … Europe is incomplete without Britain and we

> in Britain are incomplete without Europe. Therefore we wish to play our full part in this great development ... Never at any time have we hidden the fact that these political issues loom foremost in these decisions ... If we are going to face up to the fundamental problem of the political relationship of Britain with Europe, we must also face up to these other questions being openly discussed of the use of sovereignty and the best use to which we can devote it in the modern world.

After de Gaulle's veto in 1963, Heath was shattered but defiant and confident his time would come. He wrote emotional letters to the many supporters of UK accession on the Continent. To Paul-Henri Spaak he wrote the following:

> It is difficult to express one's feelings on occasions such as this ... but I wanted to say that I am very conscious of the special debt of gratitude which we owe you for everything you have done over the long months of the negotiations ... I need hardly add that we do not regard the suspension of the negotiations as the final word. We shall do everything we can to continue our work for true European unity.

A decade later, Britain's accession to the EEC was a remarkable personal triumph for Heath. Some contemporary accounts suggest he was unwisely insensitive to the feeling among many of his fellow Tories that they had been manoeuvred or even coerced into backing him. The notional 'free vote' for Conservative MPs in the crucial division that settled the matter on

28 October 1971 certainly did embolden sixty-nine Labour MPs to defy their own three-line party whip and support accession, but on the Conservative side the vote had, in reality, been heavily organised and policed by the party whips. He closed his speech on that historic day in visionary terms: 'I want Britain as a member of a Europe which is united politically, and which will enjoy lasting peace and the greater security which would ensue.'

When Heath lost power in March 1974, the scale of the blow to him personally is impossible to overstate. He personally loathed Harold Wilson, who had many of the vital qualities he lacked – human empathy (or at least the appearance of it), a deftness of touch and a chameleon-like quality that could manage a divided party with little or no obvious effort. He was also a fine communicator who easily mastered the new and already all-important medium of television, unlike Heath. Wilson was, in my view, a complete agnostic on Europe, regarding it principally as a challenge in terms of party management. (Andrew Adonis takes a different view in his essay on Wilson.) By the time Wilson's government, with its wafer-thin parliamentary majority, had completed its alleged 'renegotiation' of the terms of UK membership and called a referendum on those terms, Heath was no longer leader of the Conservative Party. For a time he had the look of a broken man, but public opinion was uncertain on the question of UK membership and the renewed call to arms had a remarkably invigorating effect on him.

Heath campaigned tirelessly in the 1975 referendum campaign and delivered some of his very best speeches, full of passion and commitment. He was also far more explicit than most people now realise on the fundamentally political nature of the European project. In the House of Commons, he set out a radical position on the knotty question of national sovereignty:

> Whether one is discussing national sovereignty or parliamentary sovereignty, what matters is the purpose of sovereignty. To me, sovereignty is not something to be hoarded, sterile and barren, carefully protected by [Enoch Powell] in a greatcoat with its collar turned up. Nor is sovereignty something which has to be kept in the crypt to be inspected.
>
> Sovereignty is something for us as custodians to use in the interests of our own country. The question we have to decide, therefore, in carrying through this great political purpose, as I believe it to be, for the peace and freedom of Europe and of our own country, is how we are entitled to use that measure of sovereignty which is required … I answer without hesitation that the sacrifice of sovereignty, if it be put in that extreme form, or the sharing of sovereignty, the transfer of sovereignty or the offering of sovereignty, is fully justified. Indeed, were we not to do so in the modern world, I believe that as a Parliament, as a party and as a government we should be culpable in the eyes of history. I believe, therefore, that sovereignty is for this House to use in the way it thinks best.

Out on the campaign trail, Heath was no less candid or provocative. In a speech made on 25 April, he declared:

> Of course, a country, like an individual, can decide to go it

> alone. And in theory at least, they may appear to have more freedom. But freedom to do what? Free to buy what you want – but too poor to afford it. Free to say whatever you like – but too weak for anyone to listen … This is the sovereignty and the freedom that the anti-Marketeers dangle before you – but it is a sham sovereignty and a fictional freedom.

While in Edinburgh on 22 May, he stated that:

> [In 1957] six nations took part in the historic step of founding the European Economic Community. This was much more than a common market. It was a community in the real sense of the word, going well beyond a customs union. It was a positive act of genuine political cooperation.

And during an appearance on BBC Radio 4, Heath explained:

> What I have always said … is that we shall 'pool' part of our sovereignty with that of other countries; and they pool theirs with us, and we do this because it's in our interest for the benefits which we get … It is the first time in British history that we have had a say over the sovereignty of eight other countries in Europe … I've always used the expression 'pooling' sovereignty because it is, in fact, describing the exact position. I believe sovereignty is something we should use and use it for the advantage of our fellow citizens.

Heath could have been a lot less open than he was about the

political implications of European unity. He was extremely unusual in being so outspokenly honest. Yet the tired old question of whether Heath had dissembled, or partially concealed the truth, or simply lied, came to a head again at the 1997 general election – Heath's last – at which the Referendum Party, led by Sir James Goldsmith, predicated its entire platform on the allegation that the people of Britain had been sold a pup in the referendum of 1975. I remember Heath's outrage when it transpired that his former economic adviser from his time as Prime Minister, Brian Reading, was to stand against him in Old Bexley and Sidcup as the Referendum Party candidate. Above Brian Reading's signature in one piece of campaign literature appeared the following:

> Joining the single currency is a step on to a bus, made in Maastricht, driven by Brussels, destination the Fourth Reich. Sir Edward Heath wants to push us on. The Lib-Dems wish us to board voluntarily. Labour wants on, but dare not say so. In Old Bexley and Sidcup I alone say, 'Let the bus leave without us.'

When I met him during that campaign, Brian Reading told me he had accepted the invitation to stand because, had he not, there would have been far more animus in the Bexley campaign and 'I didn't want to see Ted get hurt.' I tried to intercede with Heath and explain Brian's motives. He swatted me away. For my book marking Heath's centenary in 2016, Brian filled in more of the gaps:

> I had no angst against Heath, [we] just disagreed over Europe.

> I campaigned for just three weeks, going round in a van with a loud speaker on top – 'Save the pound, vote Reading'. To my horror, the referendum campaign launched a vitriolic personal attack on Heath. I had no hand in this. I therefore made a speech addressing the accusation that Heath had lied when taking us into the then European Economic Community. They claimed he had deliberately pretended that British sovereignty had not been handed to Brussels.
>
> I argued that, in his view, this was not any lie. In 1973, it was a common market not a European Union. Brussels laws were made by councils of ministers and required unanimity. Any minister could veto any law. Sovereignty had been given away, but not by Westminster to Brussels. It was given away from Parliament to government ministers: ministerial meetings were then conducted in secret without any information on who voted for what. I believe nobody paid any attention to my speech. It would have been better if I had pulled out as a candidate. That would have got attention.

Brian Reading held an open meeting in the election campaign on the question: 'Did Edward Heath Lie?' Anyone hoping he would denounce his old boss as a serial mendicant was, however, disappointed. As he confirmed to me in 2016, 'It was my intention to disappoint those baying for Ted's blood … Ted's position was totally understandable given his experience and generation. He was not dishonest, but to my mind mistaken, given the way things developed. Ted had many faults, but he was genuine.'

So what is Heath's legacy? The principal element of it – UK

membership of the EU – is being dismembered in the wake of the 2016 referendum. The European Union became, in the minds of too many voters, synonymous with the smugness, arrogance and nepotism that have polluted too much of public life, so Heath's dogged campaign to take the UK into the European Community might ultimately be judged a failure.

• • •

This essay was among Heath's papers at the time of his death. It has never before been published. It appears to date from around 1990, the time he began work on a mooted book that he had planned to write about Europe. It may well have been written for that.

The Inauguration of the Community

The initial drive for the creation of a European Community came basically from the recognition of the fact that the Council of Europe was not a suitable means for creating the European unity that so many desired. With the League of Nations in mind, it was recognised that the Council was a means of exchanging views which could affect the policies of individual countries, but it had in the ultimate event, no effective way of preventing conflict between them. Combined with this was a desire to increase rapidly the development of the European economies, especially those of the previously occupied territories. It was for this reason that Belgium, Holland and Luxembourg had combined together on 5 September 1944.

The Tariff Union of Benelux, as they came to be known colloquially, came into force on 1 January 1948.

After he left Washington at the end of the war, Jean Monnet returned to Paris where, with a handful of helpers, he worked out the plan for the reconstruction of the French economy. He secured President de Gaulle's backing for this and it provided the basis for the French economic recovery. No one realised better than Jean Monnet, however, that the German economy was also rapidly re-establishing itself in the industrial sphere. Monnet therefore wished to find a means by which Germany's industrial strength could be prevented from overwhelming the economies of France and the Benelux countries. In particular, he recognised that coal and steel were the two basic industries which had to be kept in balance.

At the same time each of the two major countries had opportunities to offer the other. The basic question from the French point of view was therefore how an economically expanding Germany could be kept under control. It ought also to have been the concern of the British government.

Jean Monnet, again with just a handful of helpers, set about producing another plan for this purpose. Its essence was to put the coal and steel industries of France and Germany, and of any other country who cared to join them, under the supranational authority. This authority would control the production of the two materials essential for manufacturing the weapons of war. It would prevent either from embarking on the manufacture of armaments unbeknown to its neighbour and thus putting itself in a position once again of waging war against it. It was this plan that Monnet took to Monsieur Bidault, the French Prime Minister, in the spring of 1950. What happened after that was described to me by Jean Monnet. Robert Schumann, the French Foreign Minister, sent his Chef de Cabinet, to whom Monnet had mentioned the plan, to enquire what had happened to it. Monnet replied that he had taken it to the Prime Minister, but had heard nothing since. Monnet then went to the Prime Minister's office and enquired from his Chef de Cabinet where the plan was, to which he received the reply, 'in the third drawer down in Bidault's desk'. Monnet asked him to retrieve it and then took it to Schumann, who approved it, adding the sentence, 'Europe will not be built all at once or as a single whole; it will be built by concrete achievements which first create de facto solidarity.' This showed remarkable foresight as to the way in which the Community would develop by means of consistent large leaps forward.

The French Cabinet approved the plan, as did Chancellor Adenauer and the German Cabinet. Both announced their acceptance of the plan at the same time. It has always been known as the Schumann Plan, although, if the French Prime Minister had not left it in the third drawer down in his desk, it might well have been christened the Bidault Plan. There followed a period of discussion with other countries as to which of them wished to join in implementing the plan. Benelux and Italy indicated that they wished to do so. The British attitude was, first of all, coloured by an unfortunate misunderstanding that led to their belief that as Dean Acheson, the American Secretary of State, had been taken into their confidence by the French in Paris on his way to London, the plan was an anti-British arrangement contrived by the French and the Americans.

However, the British attitude was finally determined by a number of other factors which loomed large in the minds of the leading figures in the then Labour government.

The French had made it absolutely plain that they welcomed the adherence of the governments of other countries to the plan. They were invited to take part in the discussions *en principe*. This is a common enough approach on the mainland of Europe, but it was foreign to the British. To the French and the Germans it meant that they entered the discussions wishing them to be successful in achieving their objective, but reserving the right not to accept the final result if it proved unsatisfactory to them. The British, however, insisted on knowing all the details of the proposed agreement before indicating whether or not they were prepared to take part in any discussions about it. Looking back, I can see *en principe* has bedevilled every negotiation in which the British have been involved in the Community, and never more so than in the last ten years. Here is an intellectual point on which the British must come into line with other partners in the Community. There is nothing to be lost and everything to be gained by putting ourselves into the same intellectual mould as our partners.

There were, however, other matters of major importance

to the Labour government. First, they apparently believed – and feared – that the other governments involved in the discussions and later in the proposed Coal and Steel Community, would all be Christian democratic governments of the centre right. Consequently, the organisation would have no place in a socialist government embarking for the first time on carrying through rapid and major socialist changes in the United Kingdom. There were, of course, no grounds for this belief. The countries of Europe before the Second World War had had governments of many different hues. Nor was the post-war world to be any different. As history has shown, the countries of the Community have ranged from Christian democratic on the right through coalitions with a variety of different parties to Socialist ones on the left. Communist members have been involved in some in Italy and France, though the voting strength of the Communist Party has now been greatly diminished. It is ironic, however, that the Labour government's fears of forty years ago have been echoed by Mrs Thatcher in her reference to 'Marxist proposals' put forward by the president of the Commission, who is certainly no Marxist, and her statement that 'having rolled back the boundaries of socialism in her term of office', she was not going to be overwhelmed by them in the Community, again a threat of which there is no possibility whatsoever.

Secondly, the Labour government believed that the proposed Community would prohibit public ownership at a time when it had carried through a massive programme of the nationalisation of the major industries in Britain, and would only support private ownership. This, too, was a hallucination. The treaties on which the Community is founded have always accepted both public and private ownership, stipulating, however, that the treatment of each, particularly in the field of financial subsidies, must be fair. There was also strong objection among the leading members of the Labour government to the idea of a supranational authority controlling some aspects of the country's economic life even though they were very ready to welcome it in the case of France and Germany.

Again we must pause for a moment's reflection at this point. When the three communities, the Coal and Steel Community, Euratom and the Economic Community, were combined in 1965 the supranational powers of the Coal and Steel Community were, of course, maintained and combined with the powers of the other authorities in the European Community itself. Thus, when the British government boasts that the British steel industry has again begun to make a profit after losses over a period of fifteen years, it must recognise that it is doing so under a supranational authority.

The Labour government finally decided not to take part in the discussions and the negotiations went ahead without them. I once asked Jean Monnet whether he was not bitterly disappointed at this point. 'No', he replied rather wearily, 'just somewhat depressed. But I always said to myself that when the British realised that the whole thing was a success they would ask to join, and', he added, looking me in the face, 'here you are.'

Looking back, of course, one can discern other factors that

consciously or unconsciously affected the Labour government's decision and indeed a great deal of public opinion in the country and in all parties at the time. There was the very powerful psychological factor that we British were the victors in the Second World War, and we were dealing with the vanquished or those who had been defeated and then rescued by us. There was, therefore, no reason why the British would need to take part in any of these proposed activities, although it was a welcome sight to see the other countries doing so. This, of course, showed no appreciation of what the impact would be of a united Europe on the mainland with Britain outside it. Gone would be the historic role, maintained by Britain over centuries, of setting out to achieve a balance of power between the major countries of the mainland. Britain could have no influence on the rest of a united Europe by staying outside it.

There were then, of course, the connections with the Commonwealth and the colonies, much to the fore as a result of their support during the Second World War. As part of this connection was the economic protectionism arising from the Ottawa Agreements of 1932, during the world economic crisis. It appeared to have served Britain well for nearly twenty years, and in the short term, throughout the '30s, may well have done so. In the long term, however, it is now apparent that it hindered the development of a modern industrial base and technology for the British. If we could go on selling old goods to a great colonial empire that had no alternative sources of supply, why should we change them? When we took large food supplies from Canada, Australia and New Zealand were we not entitled to expect them automatically to take British manufactured goods? As a result, there was no incentive to the British to move forward with the times as the United States and some European countries were doing.

There appeared to be no inkling in the minds of the British that the era of the great colonial powers was rapidly approaching its end. Despite the emergence of India, Pakistan and Ceylon as independent members of the Commonwealth from the subcontinent of colonial India, despite the Dutch and the French being forced from their territories, we should within a decade have started on the path of providing complete independence to the greater part of our colonial empire. No one recognised that with the disappearance of our empire, Britain would be left alone both politically and economically unless it were to help rebuild its own continent. Other colonial powers showed greater appreciation of a rapidly developing situation and withdrew as amicably as possible in order to keep close and friendly relations with their former territories.

Another feature of the situation was the belief that Britain was inexorably tied to the United States, not only by past history, but also by the immense debt which they had incurred to the Americans during the Second World War, by the various defence arrangements between the two countries in the West Indies. It was true that President Truman and the American Congress, the war having finished, immediately cut Britain off from all sources of atomic and nuclear information, despite the fact that the work had been jointly carried out during the war. However, with the arrival of Mr Churchill at 10 Downing Street and General Eisenhower at the White House, the relations in the defence field certainly improved, only to re-emphasise the dependence of Britain on the United States of America.

The overall view of British foreign policy at this time was clearly demonstrated by Sir Anthony Eden, when, as Foreign Secretary in 1952, he described the world situation as consisting of three interlocking circles, the Commonwealth, Europe and the Atlantic Alliance. He then went on to point out that Britain was at the centre of all three concentric circles. This bolstered the feeling in the Conservative Party at that time and to a certain extent in public opinion in the country that Britain was still on its own a leading world power. It was ironic that this view was demolished by the Suez operation during Sir Anthony Eden's premiership three years later.

Finally, there was a deep-seated belief that, if the rest of Europe could solve its problems on its own, it would no longer be likely to interfere with us in Britain. The British could then happily carry on in their own way. Alas, this also proved to be illusory. When the countries of the mainland of Europe did show they could solve their own problems peacefully, improve the standard of living of their peoples and embark on a period of stability and prosperity, it became all too obvious that Britain would have to do the same. In 1973, we became a member of the Community. It had cost us nearly twenty-five years as outsiders. So the six member countries – France, Germany, Italy, Belgium, the Netherlands and Luxembourg – created the Coal and Steel Community as the foundation stone for European unity. Its purpose was political: to stop France and Germany ever fighting each other again.

Never must this be forgotten. Its purpose remains political. With the rapidly changing face of Eastern Europe, it becomes ever more important to remember this fact. The means of achieving the political purpose was and still is economic. It is by improving the standard of living of its people and providing a period of stability and prosperity that the Community overcomes the dangers of European conflicts. It is this that has attracted those who have been fighting for freedom in the countries of Eastern Europe. It is this which can help them to free and peaceful societies in the future.

CHAPTER 8

JAMES CALLAGHAN

DAVID OWEN

'Non, merci beaucoup.'

James Callaghan rejecting a 'French-led Europe' in Southampton, May 1971

Callaghan served in the Royal Navy during the war, but after being elected to Parliament as a Labour MP in July 1945, his first major exposure to European issues was in 1947, when he attended the new Council of Europe in Strasbourg. In August 1949, he was deputising for Herbert Morrison, who had urged him to ensure that the other member nations adopted British parliamentary procedures. Unsurprisingly, he had failed as all the other members of the Council of Europe were insistent on adopting their more familiar Continental practice. In Strasbourg, all the big figures – Monnet, Mollet, Schumann and Spaak – attended.

The British delegation were adamantly against a European army. Schumann's announcement in 1950, proposing a European Steel and Coal Community, was opposed by Ernest Bevin who argued that its real purpose was to bind France and Germany together economically and ultimately militarily, while keeping Britain at a distance. 'They don't want us, Callaghan', he said pronouncing his name incorrectly with a hard g. Callaghan, addressing the European Consultative Assembly in Strasbourg, said:

> We regard ourselves as part of Europe. We desire to work with Europe and our intention and aim is that there should be the fullest cooperation between us all. Today all of us are interdependent. I must remind those who advocate a federal arrangement for Europe that theirs is not the only method by which sovereignty can be pooled and merged into something larger.

After the 1950 election, Callaghan, who had been Parliamentary Secretary to the Minister of Transport since 1947, became Parliamentary Secretary to the Royal Navy. When Labour lost the Election in 1951, Callaghan shadowed Transport. On Europe he surprisingly supported Aneurin Bevan against German rearmament. After Attlee retired, Callaghan supported Hugh Gaitskell as leader and supported him over the Suez invasion. Europe featured less when he became colonial and Commonwealth spokesman, during which time Callaghan travelled extensively, particularly in Africa. According to Callaghan's biographer,

Kenneth Morgan, by 1962 Callaghan and Gaitskell 'saw matters very much as one', with Gaitskell coming out strongly in his October conference speech against Prime Minister Macmillan's application for membership of the European Economic Community (EEC).

> Both the appeals to history and to ties with Commonwealth countries were entirely congenial to Callaghan who was no great Euro-enthusiast now ... He told the Edmonton Labour Party that any move towards federalism would threaten the British identity. 'If we join Europe we cut ourselves adrift from much of the Commonwealth by the very act of accepting the Treaty of Rome.'

Callaghan served in government from 1964 to 1970, first as Chancellor of the Exchequer and then as Home Secretary under Harold Wilson, who he had run against for the leadership after Gaitskell's death in January 1963. While Wilson was leader, Callaghan supported his attempt to join the European Community.

Yet after Edward Heath's victory in 1970, Labour started slowly to make the European Community an issue for opposition as evidenced, when, on 19 January 1971, a straight anti-EEC motion received 119 signatures from Labour MPs, with the number eventually rising to 132. Labour pro-marketeers countered this by launching a European Declaration with Willy Brandt, the former German Chancellor. On 11 May, we had 100 Labour MPs signing up for a *Guardian* advertisement, the most prominent being Roy Jenkins, Denis Healey and Anthony Crosland. I was chosen to approach Jim Callaghan and I rang him while he was on his farm in Sussex, having got his number from his son-in-law, Peter Jay. It was the first time I had ever negotiated directly with him and in doing so I got a sense of the formidable strengths he had developed in the 1930s, as a trade union official.

Eventually, we agreed a formula acceptable to both of us. He would say that 'he had been approached, but refused to sign on the grounds that it was better for the shadow Cabinet members to stay outside such an initiative. He had not, in consequence, been given the wording of the declaration, which meant that he had no view on it.' Of course, I had told him what was in the declaration, but our agreed formula meant he couldn't now brief the press to say the statement was innocuous and downplay the whole initiative, which would have been very damaging. The whole experience left me with a new respect for him.

The Heath–Pompidou breakthrough negotiation meeting ended on 21 May 1971. Just four days later, the pro-market Labour cause was dealt a major blow. Jim Callaghan made his devastating 'Language of Chaucer' speech at a by-election in Southampton. His '*non, merci beaucoup*' comment made it clear that he believed the Labour Party should reject entry. Picking up on Pompidou's reference to French as the language of Europe, he declared shamelessly, 'Millions of people in Britain have been surprised to hear that the language of Chaucer, Shakespeare and Milton must in future be regarded as an American import from which we must protect ourselves if we are to build a new Europe.'

There was, however, one very perceptive passage in his speech that anticipated the controversy of why the euro currency meant a federalist Europe:

> I understand there is to be a confederation of member states whose ministers will retain full powers of decision. That is to say, they can disagree with decisions taken by other countries and so can prevent action by the EEC countries. This is a contradictory position for, if there is to be a successful economic and monetary union, then member states will have to subordinate their own fiscal, taxation and monetary policies to a central governing body.

There is every reason to believe that if Jim Callaghan had supported entry and not made that speech, Harold Wilson would not have come out against the terms of the negotiations. Wilson firmed up his opposition when he was told of Jim's comment to a senior Lobby journalist not willing to go to Southampton: 'Well, if you want to hear the next Leader of the Labour Party, you'd better arrange to be there.' Callaghan had done much the same with his opposition to Barbara Castle and Wilson's trade union reform package in 1969, 'In Place of Strife'. Once again, Callaghan was putting himself at the vanguard of mainstream Labour Party opinion and as a consequence Denis Healey and Anthony Crosland also began to move their positions on Europe too.

Callaghan never disguised his belief that Labour MPs, like me, should not have voted in principle for EEC membership but should instead have kept to the party line. He wrote in his autobiography that we had opened up a 'deep rift' by going 'into the Yes Lobby with the government whilst the great majority of the party marched with the rest of the shadow Cabinet into the No Lobby, declaring that they were not against the principle of membership but were dissatisfied with the terms'.

It was Callaghan who saw the potential for unifying the party around Tony Benn's suggested referendum, describing the idea as a 'life raft' aboard which the warring factions could clamber. As Foreign Secretary after Labour had won both the February and October general elections of 1974, Callaghan faced, over the referendum on the EEC, in his own words:

> The hard task of yoking together horses which were pulling in opposite directions and this might have resulted in the carriage lurching so uncontrollably from side to side that it overturned the government … I found myself corresponding with the Chancellor, Denis Healey, about import levels of apricot halves and canned fruit salad, and with Peter Shore about mutton and lamb. I recall one low point when nine Foreign Ministers from the major countries of Europe solemnly assembled in Brussels to spend several hours discussing how to resolve our differences on standardising a fixed position of rear-view mirrors on agricultural tractors. I wondered what Palmerston, Salisbury or Bevin would have made of it, and

> sometimes I grumbled to my officials that I felt not so much a Foreign Secretary as a multiple grocer.

Helmut Schmidt, the German Chancellor, was the critical factor in arguing that Britain had made out a case for its net contribution to be modified and Germany was ready to support the formula drawn up by the Commission. It was not enough, but the concession clinched the deal and Schmidt proposed a maximum refund of 250 million units of account, equivalent to about £125 million in any one year. Getting a better financial deal was a constant theme of Callaghan's premiership and it was eventually conceded to Mrs Thatcher as Prime Minister. For Callaghan, the 1975 referendum was not about sovereignty in contrast to the wish to take back control in 2016. Nor was it about the Commonwealth. During the referendum campaign, a senior civil servant, Patrick Nairn, wrote to Callaghan who with Wilson had made it clear they would implement the result even if it was not what they recommended, to the effect that in the event of a 'No' vote there would be no need to hurry into a withdrawal. Callaghan contradicted him in the most powerful terms, arguing that it would be necessary to start repealing the 1972 Act very soon thereafter.

Callaghan claimed that after the referendum at the party conference in 1975, 'not a single reference to the bitter dispute that had split and divided the party for fifteen years' was made. But by 1980 the same dispute returned with a vengeance and Labour by 1981, when the SDP was launched, was committed to coming out of the EEC without even a referendum. It was Callaghan's considerable achievement to convert many Labour MPs and voters to an acceptance of British membership of the European Community for six years from 1974 to 1980. He managed this successfully because he too was on a journey from sceptic to supporter, which in later life became full-hearted support.

On Boxing Day 1975, Harold Lever telephoned Callaghan, at Wilson's request, to let him know that Wilson planned to resign in March. Roy Jenkins told me some days later that he too had been told Wilson would resign within a few months. Callaghan, with the help of Merlyn Rees, immediately started to run a very professional, well-judged but quiet campaign. The Jenkins campaign, by contrast, reflected the ambivalence of the candidate who had already privately told Wilson in late January, after initially rejecting Wilson's offer of becoming President of the European Commission, that he would like to be considered. On the third ballot, on 5 April 1976, Callaghan beat Michael Foot by 176 to 137 votes. In the *Financial Times*, David Watt, my best political friend, summed Callaghan up as a supreme politician, a highly capable negotiator and conciliator, and a good salesman for Britain – although his weaknesses were on policy and his sense of insecurity. Having personally voted for Jenkins with deepening disappointment and for Healey with affection and admiration, I voted for Callaghan on the third ballot, as I believed he was the only person who could navigate the government through the troubled waters ahead.

The Prime Minister's first task was to choose his Cabinet. Michael Foot wanted and got the job of Leader of the House of Commons. Callaghan was aware of Roy's interest in becoming

President of the European Commission, a post that would commence on 1 January 1977, so he kept Roy as Home Secretary, holding open the prospect of moving to being Chancellor but never considered him to be Foreign Secretary. He judged that every action Roy took as Foreign Secretary would be looked on with suspicion by the anti-marketeers on the backbenches. Tony Crosland had been close to Jim Callaghan for many years and would have liked to succeed Denis Healey as Chancellor, but due to the impending financial crisis, Jim believed there was no change possible there. Biographer Kenneth Morgan reveals, much to my surprise, that Callaghan had even then considered appointing me Foreign Secretary, but I continued as Minister of Health while he removed Barbara Castle as Secretary of State for Health and Social Security. In September of that year, he appointed me as Crosland's deputy and Minister for Europe, implying I could expect to come into the Cabinet when the UK presidency of the European Community was over at the end of June 1977. Tragically, Tony died in February 1977, following a severe brain haemorrhage and much to my surprise I took over as Foreign Secretary.

The handling of the International Monetary Fund (IMF) crisis, far more than Europe, was the making of Callaghan as Prime Minister. On his first day in office, Callaghan was told that sterling, which stood at an exchange rate of $1.86 and falling, might fall by 10–15 per cent. On 12 April, Healey told him that the Bank of England had spent $2 billion in support of sterling over the last fifteen months. I was not a member of the Cabinet that wrestled with the IMF's demands, but I had a ringside seat from the Foreign Office since Tony Crosland shared his thinking about why the IMF demands for public expenditure cuts should be resisted. Healey knew what had to be done because, unlike Crosland, he understood it was all a matter of retaining international confidence. Callaghan understood we had lost the confidence of Walter Simon, the Head of the US Treasury and Arthur Burns, chair of the US Federal Reserve. He challenged Johannes Witteveen, the Dutch head of the IMF, and used his personal links to obtain some softening of the position from direct talks with Helmut Schmidt, Henry Kissinger and President Ford. Yet there was no further give and Callaghan understood that. He steered the three-way Cabinet divide with exemplary skill and patience. He kept a one-on-one dialogue with Witteveen, which Healey knew about right to the end. On 9 December, Healey announced the IMF loan of £3.9 billion.

A bizarre aspect of Callaghan's tenure, which much exercised the federalists in all their different guises in the first half of 1977, was the 'War of Jenkins's Seat' and whether the President of the Commission should attend the G7 meeting in London that summer and which, rather embarrassingly, coincided with the UK presidency. This war was of shorter duration than the more famous 'War of Jenkins's Ear' that took place from 1739 to 1748. One of the joys of working with Callaghan as Foreign Secretary was that wherever possible he made sure we travelled together, something that I've noticed my successors have done rather infrequently. Apart from time for a good gossip, it afforded me the opportunity to catch up on the domestic political pressures and, above all, it was a time for me to learn from Jim's experience.

Jim was adamant from the start that Roy Jenkins, as President of the European Commission, should not attend the G7 meeting, arguing that it was creating a bad precedent, not having happened before. There was substance involved as well as ego. European federalists then, as now, lost no opportunity to boost the pretension that the EU has the status of a country and deserves representation in its own right. In those days, there was no common foreign and security policy, let alone any attempt at a European defence policy; that was all to come in the wake of the European Constitution presented in 2003, which despite being rejected by the French and Dutch in referendums in 2005 was reinstated in the infamous Treaty of Lisbon signed in 2007 and ratified in 2009.

Not unreasonably Roy Jenkins wanted to mark his presidency with increased recognition for the standing of the President of the Commission and again, not unreasonably, Holland and Belgium and some other members of the nine-country EEC were keen for this to happen so they could bring some influence on the G7 of the US, UK, France, Germany, Italy, Canada and Japan. Italy kept quiet, pleased to be a member of the G7 in their own right. I tried to dissuade Jim from taking this line, thinking it a reasonable request, and feared a rather undignified row. I also thought it would bring up old animosities between Roy and Jim and far better to let the French President Giscard d'Estaing make the running in opposing in principle the proposal. Jim and I discussed it always without any civil servants or diplomats present and he was implacable. I promised to do my best to block it.

On 8 March, I chaired a restricted session of my first meeting of the Foreign Affairs Council. The French Foreign Minister, Louis de Guiringaud, said under instruction from Giscard that the French were against. I said the presidency had no view. After some discussion around the Council, with Roy arguing strongly for representation, I did my duty by Jim and summed up that since there was no consensus, the Council would agree that the President of the Commission would not be represented. Roy objected, arguing that it was too soon to close the debate down and so it went on in public for months to no one's real advantage. Schmidt had told Callaghan that privately he had been against Jenkins attending. Callaghan and I then flew by Concorde to Washington to meet with President Jimmy Carter. Since we held the presidency of the EU, Callaghan, though under no obligation to do so, asked the President's opinion on the matter of whether Jenkins should have a seat in the meeting due to take place in May, making it clear that he did not favour Roy's attendance but adding in a generous way, as I was sitting beside him, that I was of a different view.

Despite Carter indicating his preference for Jenkins to be present, Jim did not change his view, although he softened a bit. A compromise was eventually reached that meant Jenkins would not be present when matters unrelated to the Commission were discussed. Naturally, I was never able to tell Roy or fellow EEC ministers that actually I had always been in favour of him being present. Giscard, who never weakened his stance, refused to come to the dinner at No. 10 on the eve of the formal meeting if Roy was present. Jim shrugged his shoulders and resigned himself to Giscard not being there and accepted personal defeat with grace. It is a small story, but behind the vanities was the permanent struggle of the Jean Monnet wish for a federal Europe which Callaghan at this stage was more aware of than I.

On Europe itself, the most important long-term issue was Callaghan's handling of the Exchange Rate Mechanism (ERM). The European Council meeting at Copenhagen on 8 April 1978 provided Callaghan and Giscard d'Estaing with an opportunity to hear about Schmidt's idea of a European-type Bretton Woods, with a European exchange rate fixed against the dollar, which would effectively mean Europe becoming a Deutsche Mark zone. D'Estaing, despite some cosmetic criticisms, had clearly worked closely on it with Schmidt. Callaghan explained why the proposals disadvantaged Britain, for the strong Deutsche Mark would have the effect of tugging sterling upwards with deflationary consequences for the British economy, unless long-term credit was absolutely unlimited. Nevertheless, Callaghan favoured the general idea as likely to bring more order into the currency markets of Europe and the world. Quite apart from his technical concerns he knew many in the Cabinet would be suspicious of what they thought was too close an entanglement with Europe. Cleverly, Callaghan kept his options open when, some days later, he told Schmidt and d'Estaing that we could not enter the European Monetary Scheme (EMS) at the outset.

On Africa, Callaghan had built up personal friendships over the decades with many Commonwealth heads of government and was hugely supportive of my endeavours, particularly over the civil war in Southern Rhodesia. He passed a note across the table during a Cabinet meeting on 21 September to ask if I would have lunch with him at the Athenaeum. Prime Ministers are automatically given membership of this club, though Jim hardly ever used it. We were due to fly out to Kano in Nigeria the next day to meet the Zimbabwean President Kenneth Kaunda, who had telephoned Jim in a near hysterical mood after Rhodesian Prime Minister Ian Smith's armed forces had invaded the outskirts of his capital city, Lusaka. He was threatening to buy weapons from the then Soviet Union and demanding the two should meet. They settled at meeting a few days later in Kano. Typically, Jim had phoned me to apologise for fixing up the meeting without consulting me and insisted on my flying out with him. Prime Ministers do not appear these days to have such a courteous relationship with their Foreign Secretaries.

We used the lunch, accompanied by Ken Stowe, his principal private secretary, to think through our strategy. After our meal, Jim decided to walk back to Parliament through St James's Park and he motioned to Ken to hang back so that we could talk privately about Denis Healey. He then brought up the issue of the EMS and his concern about two speeches that Healey had made recently, one of which appeared to argue that we should join the ERM. Jim reiterated his view that the party would not wear entry to the ERM and that it would have to wait until after the election. I suggested the possibility advanced recently to me by a diplomat, Michael Butler, of joining the EMS but not the ERM. Jim pondered this for a moment and then asked me what Healey's attitude might be and I said he could be persuaded. Then, Callaghan, ever fertile in man management, suggested that I get Butler to square the Treasury officials who could sell this somewhat ingenious approach to Healey who could bring it to Cabinet as his idea and he would appease Peter Shore. At the subsequent Cabinet discussion, Healey and Callaghan argued that we wanted a zone of monetary stability and that we should commit ourselves to helping to achieve this, but without any obligations restricting our own freedom to manage the sterling exchange rate as we thought fit. I was doubtful whether any of the other Cabinet members, except Harold Lever and Peter Shore, understood what was happening and that we would not join the ERM, the element in the EMS to which Peter was most adamantly opposed, but we would join the monetary system.

Later, Parliament agreed that we would be associated with the development of the European Currency Unit (ECU) and the UK made up our national share of gold deposits and committed dollar reserves. This ensured that the ECU had sufficient backing from all nine countries. The advantage for the European Community of this compromise was that the necessary procedural hurdles were passed by the Labour government for full membership at a later date. When, under a Conservative government, Britain joined the ERM in October 1990, no new authority was required and entry was fixed up quickly and conveniently over the weekend. Yet its flaws, which Callaghan spotted were never fully addressed, led inexorably to the UK pulling out.

Given the nature of the split Cabinet on European questions

and the parliamentary party attitudes at the end of 1978, we could not have got any closer to being a full member of the EMS; it was a considerable achievement to have come as far as the UK did and an important gesture towards European solidarity. Of course the 'closet' euro federalists among diplomats and some politicians in the Labour and Conservative parties attributed little or no credit to Callaghan personally. The Treasury were strongly supportive, however, and they were never enthusiastic about the ERM as it developed. Callaghan's approach was mirrored later in the Maastricht Treaty by Prime Minister John Major in that we did opt out of the euro, but did not stop other EU states from having to join. Denmark later adopted our approach. At a meeting in Paris, Giscard d'Estaing presented Callaghan, Healey and me with the first minted ECU – and I am still in possession of one, a reminder of the euro. The Maastricht Treaty, a federalist measure, was something, in retrospect, the UK should have vetoed if we were to avoid laying the foundation for Brexit.

Another federalist measure was direct elections for the European Assembly, as it was initially named, though it was clearly destined to be called a Parliament. It was pushed through a reluctant Cabinet and Parliament. The one major achievement we ensured was that no increase in the powers of the European Parliament which required unanimity could ever be pushed through by late-night pressure on UK ministers to sign up. Instead, prior agreement was needed through primary legislation of the UK Parliament. The other significant accompaniment to direct elections to the European Assembly was that for the first time a majority of a UK Cabinet accepted genuine proportional representation. It was a hard fought victory agreed before the Lib–Lab pact which then included it, but only with a pledge that the Prime Minister would use his best endeavours to carry it through Parliament. Under Tony Blair, it eventually became the system of voting that currently operates and the Parliament has become de facto the body that chooses the President of the Commission.

There were many other issues resolved by agreement within the procedures of the EEC during Callaghan's period in office despite the fact that we had little enthusiasm for them. He did, however, stop the attempt to drop British Summer Time. 'Don't touch it' was his message to the Home Secretary, Merlyn Rees. We went along with a new European passport with the UK and Royal Crest being placed above the words European Community, but that order was reversed years later.

The main diplomatic achievement of Callaghan's Prime Ministership was paving the way for the enlargement of the EEC by admitting Greece, Spain and Portugal to make an EEC of twelve countries. As Foreign Secretary in the Socialist International network, Callaghan did a lot with the German Social Democratic Party (SPD) to ensure Mario Soares became Prime Minister following the Carnation Revolution, which overthrew the Portuguese Prime Minister, Marcelo Caetano. Caetano had limped on after the death of the Portuguese fascist Prime Minister, António de Oliveira Salazar, who had governed from 1932 to 1968. Salazar's regime, known as Estado Novo, had rather disreputably been accepted as a founding member of NATO in 1949.

In April 1974, the revolution, led by military officers on the left, many of them communists, took power and brought the unpopular Colonial War, involving Portuguese territories including Portuguese Guinea, São Tomé , East Timor, Mozambique and Angola, to an end. From 1974 to 1976 the Revolutionary Council ruled and it was not at all sure whether Portugal would end up a democracy. Callaghan found unconventional money and with German funds from the SPD they successfully manoeuvred so that an election in 1976 led to Mario Soares becoming Prime Minister. General Eanes served as President from 1976 to 1986 with support from the left, including the Communists, as well as the centre.

On 21 and 22 May, I was host at Leeds Castle in Kent at the traditional weekend meeting of Foreign Secretaries and the President of the Commission. We all accepted the strong political case for enlargement of the Community to include Spain and Portugal in addition to Greece, who had already made a formal application. From that moment on there was a tussle over whether Greece should be admitted with no obligation towards Spanish and Portuguese entry, as preferred by France which was given lukewarm support by the Commission, both being worried about the impact of more Mediterranean products such as oranges, tomatoes and other agricultural products including wine. The issue was resolved by Schmidt and Callaghan, who were of one mind and kept confronting Giscard d'Estaing on this question on a number of occasions in 1977–78. They made it clear eventually over breakfast that unless Giscard gave them both a personal assurance that if they agreed Greece could come first, France would not block Portugal and Spain, otherwise they would block Greece. Giscard gave that assurance and France honoured that commitment. Bringing Spain into the EU helped greatly in changing Labour Party attitudes to Europe, particularly with two key Labour figures, Michael Foot, the Leader of the House of Commons, and Jack Jones, the leader of the T&GWU trade union, who had fought in the Spanish Civil War. On Portugal's entry the relationship of Schmidt and Callaghan was also pivotal. Their close relationship, continuing into semi-retirement, became a key factor in Callaghan's movement towards enthusiasm for the EU.

Our UK presidency of the European Community ended with the European Council in London on 29 to 30 June 1977. I cannot say our presidency had been a great success, but nor had it been a disaster which it might have been given the continuing divisions on Europe within the Cabinet. While some of the animosity against the Community in the Labour Party was abating, we were far from having a committed, coherent line. I strongly welcomed Jim Callaghan's decision to have a special Cabinet meeting on our European position at the end of July. He asked me to write the paper personally rather than rely on a bland draft contribution from the Department and also to ensure there were some political objectives underpinning our strategy. A day or two before the Cabinet meeting I met with a group of 'Jenkinsites' who periodically lunched with Roy. Roy had clearly been briefed about my Cabinet paper and launched characteristically into coded criticism of people who were backsliding on Europe. He objected to enlargement because it would lead to a loosening and slowing of the momentum towards greater union. In my view he now represented the European interest which did not necessarily match British interests and I argued the anti-federalist position that enlargement would give some protection from federalism but it was, above all, a democratic duty. These and other divisive issues for many people in the UK culminated in the 2016 referendum. I have never seen sovereignty as an absolute. I believe it right in NATO and the UN and some other international bodies to give up or pool some sovereignty. But the essentials of nationhood I have never believed should be eroded. The belief that it is not possible to have a single currency without becoming virtually a single nation has I believe been validated by the failures of the Eurozone.

The outcome of our all-day Cabinet meeting, which Tony Benn described in his diaries as one of the most remarkable Cabinets he had ever attended, was to have, at least for the rest of our time in government, an official policy which was firmly pro-European, anti-federalist and committed to enlargement to include Greece, Portugal and Spain. It was also committed to forcing reform of the Common Agricultural Policy through vetoing its pricing. It was Jim's task with some help from me to sell that package primarily to the Labour Party at the autumn conference in October 1977 and that we did.

Callaghan was above all a Labour trade unionist. To anyone who questions – and many do, particularly on the left of the Labour Party – Callaghan's socialism, there can be no doubt about his commitment to international socialism. First over Portugal and then after Franco died in 1975, Callaghan championed at every turn the democratic case for binding these countries into the EEC. The fact that the military did try to overthrow the Spanish government a few years later – an attempt that was halted, to his great credit, by the King – showed how fragile was the situation.

His social conscience was established with the full support of his wife, Audrey, in his championing of child policies as Home Secretary, in which capacity he established the Houghton Commission on Adoption, Fostering and Child Care and supported my Children's Bill in 1973, which eventually became an Act in 1975. Of his period as Prime Minister, he fully fulfilled the old adage that 'office maketh the man'. As the Head of the UK government he drew on his time as a trade union negotiator, but there was a new reasoned pragmatism, and he became a principled politician. There was a readiness to put country before party, an all-round solidity that few of his predecessors ever matched. He showed it when he supported, on numerous occasions in Africa, the unequivocal call for one person, one vote, when all his predecessors had shirked the responsibility. He recognised that six and a half years was far too long for a British Foreign Secretary not to visit Moscow and the USSR and supported my visit. He took a continuing interest in negotiations for the need for a Test Ban Treaty. Even on whether the UK needed to target Moscow with nuclear warheads – the so-called Moscow criteria – he showed an open mindedness and readiness to hold long and open discussions with three key Cabinet ministers. On Europe, he began a journey from agnostic in 1947, sceptic in 1970 to pragmatic support as Prime Minister. On the European Union in retirement, helped by his profound respect for the Europeanism of Helmut Schmidt, he became an enthusiast

CHAPTER 9

MARGARET THATCHER

CHARLES POWELL

'We have not successfully rolled back the frontiers of the state in Britain, only to see them reimposed at a European level, with a European superstate exercising a new dominance from Brussels.'

MARGARET THATCHER, BRUGES SPEECH,

SEPTEMBER 1988

Europe in the 1980s was not all about the European Union or European Community (EC) as it then was. As Margaret Thatcher said in her Bruges speech, 'the European Community is one manifestation of Europe's identity but not the only one'. Europe in the 1980s was much more about forcing the withdrawal of the Soviet intermediate nuclear missiles that threatened Europe's security. It was about bringing the Cold War to an end and liberating East and central Europe from Communism. It was about bringing down the Berlin Wall and reuniting

Germany. In strategic and global terms, these achievements were of greater significance for the future of the Continent than developments in the EC, which itself played only a peripheral role in them. In judging the performance of British Prime Ministers in Europe, one has to keep in mind the relative importance of the EC in that wider context. Margaret Thatcher's contribution to those historic changes in Europe of the 1980s was of considerably greater significance than her part in the EC.

In a similar vein, politics and government in the UK in the 1980s were not all about the EC as they seem to be now, when it seems almost illegal to talk about anything other than Brexit. They were about rebuilding the British economy on free market principles, reducing taxation, privatising nationalised industries, reforming industrial relations to break trade union power, re-taking the Falklands. European affairs mattered, of course they did, but not as much as the transformative changes being brought about within Britain. I would guess that Margaret Thatcher spent less time on the problems in our relations with the EC than any of her successors as Prime Minister, as well as more on changing Britain. Indeed, Europe's greatest impact on British politics of the time was, together with the poll tax, to bring down Margaret Thatcher as Prime Minister and end her political career.

I worked directly for Margaret Thatcher from 1983 to '91 and remained in touch with her thereafter. During her time as Prime Minister from 1983 onward, I attended every European meeting and every bilateral meeting with individual European leaders that she held. That gives me a claim to insight into her views, though for the period before that I have to rely mainly on what she recounted to me herself and what she and others have written. It is risky to speculate on what her view would be of Brexit, but it's fair to cite such evidence as is available from her record without actually attributing a view to her.

Margaret Thatcher had no single, consistent view of Europe throughout her political life. Just as Picasso had a Rose period, a Blue period and a Cubist period, so Margaret Thatcher's view on Europe evolved in relation to what was happening in British politics, in Continental Europe and in the wider world.

In her early life, her view was very much conditioned by the Second World War and the horrors inflicted on Europe for the second time in half a century by Germany. That's hardly surprising for a generation growing up as she did in the 1930s and '40s. It left her with an abiding concern about the re-emergence of an over-mighty Germany, a concern which outlasted reality in terms of hard power, though she was not far off the mark in foreseeing German dominance of the present-day European Union. Just ask any Italian or even Frenchman today if you doubt that.

The other conclusion she drew from the war was that while problems for Great Britain historically emerged from the Continent of Europe, salvation came from the English-speaking people of the United States and the Commonwealth. Whether that view would today have been affected by the Trump presidency one can only speculate. But it gave her a lifelong conviction that a close relationship with the United States had to be Britain's absolute priority, with Europe secondary to that.

I reject the view that her instinctive view of mainland Europe was based on ignorance of its history and of Britain's historic and cultural links with it over the centuries. You have only to read the opening paragraphs of her Bruges speech, tracing the centuries of Britain's involvement in Europe, to realise that is rubbish. Her problems were neither with history nor with our current involvement with individual European countries in almost every area of life. They were with the policies and growing powers of the supranational institutions of the EC.

Returning to my chronological account of her views, in the 1950s and early 1960s, they were characterised by disinterest shared by most other British politicians in the early steps towards creating the European Economic Community (EEC). There is no evidence of her showing interest in the Schuman Declaration or the Treaty of Rome. Her focus was unambiguously on our domestic affairs, on the Cold War and on the global threat posed by Soviet Communism. European developments outside NATO were secondary and seemed barely relevant by comparison.

But by the mid-'60s disinterest was not sustainable for a rising and ambitious junior minister and later Cabinet minister in a government and party which had decided that Britain's future lay within the European institutions. Margaret Thatcher bought into the prevailing orthodoxy and Ted Heath's enthusiasm for membership of the then EEC. She became an active member of the European Union of Women, whose goal was to 'promote European integration'. She took a prominent role in the 1975 referendum confirming our EEC membership. The high-point of her pro-EEC activity may have been the picture of her campaigning in the 1975 referendum, wearing a pullover adorned with European flags. She used to shudder at the sight of it later in life, though whether more on grounds of politics or fashion I am not sure.

She spoke in favour of European defence cooperation and criticised the then Labour government for failing to join the European Exchange Rate Mechanism (ERM). 'We underrated the advantage of the EEC,' she wrote at the time. 'I was wholly in favour of British entry into the EEC for the reasons mentioned.' Reasons in her case focused primarily on the strategic case for greater European unity and foreign policy cooperation in the face of the Soviet threat. She does not appear to have been unduly troubled at the time or indeed later, even though herself a lawyer, by the role of the European Court of Justice, which is now so central to the concerns of Brexiteers about the European Union. It would be unfair to attribute any of this to simple careerism: her views appear to be sincerely held in the context of the time.

The upshot is that Margaret Thatcher came to the leadership of the Conservative Party and then to 10 Downing Street without much of a track record on Europe. Some conventional enthusiasm for it masked considerable indifference. It's clear that she did not share Edward Heath's emotional commitment or vision, let alone that of other European leaders. Instead she had a fervent belief in Britain's capacity to manage its own affairs. She judged the EC largely by what it could contribute to her domestic policy aims. She had no overall strategy for

Britain's role in Europe or for the EC's future, and indeed never really articulated one until the Bruges Speech nearly nine years after becoming Prime Minister. As a result, her engagement with Europe became what is nowadays referred to as transactional, on a case by case basis.

But becoming Prime Minister was nonetheless a watershed. Indifference was no longer an option. She had no alternative but to engage with the EC from day one and start to confront some of the contradictions that our membership involved. Her priority was root and branch reform of the British economy through free market policies and reducing tax and regulatory burdens. Yet the ethos of the EC governments was interventionism in the economy, protectionism in foreign trade and high budgetary spending on agriculture. In foreign policy, her commitment to the special relationship with the US had to contend with the uncomfortable fact that successive American Presidents were committed to supporting European unity as a bulwark against Communist subversion and wanted Britain to be a full part of it. More fundamental still was the basic philosophical divide between intergovernmentalists and integrationists. These strategic dilemmas were accentuated by the tension between growing scepticism within the Conservative Party about the costs and constitutional constraints of our membership, and her government's stated objective to make a success of it.

None of these strategic dilemmas were resolved during Margaret Thatcher's three terms as Prime Minister or subsequently, nor could they be, as they represented irreconcilable contradictions. They could only be managed. There were, however, significant victories for British interests along the way.

The most obvious was the very substantial reduction in the cost of Britain's membership, which saved the country many billions of pounds over subsequent years. That was a plus. The negative was that it embroiled Margaret Thatcher in unremitting hostilities with the rest of the EC – Maggie battles for Britain – which embedded in her a belief that the institution was fundamentally hostile to Britain's interests, and in the rest of the members a rather sanctimonious view that Britain was incapable of being a 'good European'. This first encounter left indelible marks.

The second notable success was to complete the single market in Europe. Incredibly almost nothing had been done towards this since the Treaty of Rome was signed. Although it was not a single-handed Thatcher triumph, she provided the impetus and continuing momentum which brought immeasurable benefit to Britain, building on the success of the Big Bang in the City. It was also another example of Margaret Thatcher's transactional approach. A price had to be paid for the benefits of the single market in terms of increased qualified majority voting – without which the single market itself could never have been achieved – and a reiterated commitment to economic and monetary union that seemed pie in the sky at the time. A myth has grown up that Margaret Thatcher was conned into making this trade-off by wily pro-European British officials. The idea of Margaret Thatcher having the wool pulled over her eyes by officials is absurd in itself. Moreover, she herself never claimed it to be the case. What she did rightly object to was subsequent, and legally specious, attempts by the European Commission to extend the majority voting provisions to issues well beyond those originally envisaged, an example in her eyes of the Commission's never-ending and devious efforts to circumvent the will of national governments in the interests of increasing its own power.

I don't intend to catalogue every step of Margaret Thatcher's involvement in the European Community's affairs. There was good and bad. On the plus side of the ledger was the reduction of the proportion of the EU budget going to agriculture and – although not strictly a European Community issue – the agreement with France on the Channel Tunnel a mere couple of centuries or so from when it was first proposed. On the negative side was the steady drip of endowing the European Community with the attributes and powers of a state at the expense of individual members, which increased exponentially as economic and monetary union and then the single currency moved up the agenda.

The European Community's inability even to pause and absorb the implications and consequences of these steps to increase its powers and competencies at the expense of the member states before moving ahead with further steps increased Margaret Thatcher's frustration with the institution and the direction in which it was moving. The pitch of her indignation was caused by Jacques Delors's attendance at a TUC conference and his claim that within a short time some 80 per cent of the powers currently exercised by national governments would be in the hands of the European Community. I am not sure Delors actually said as much but that was the sense in which it was reported and believed by Margaret Thatcher.

This claim while not in itself of great importance and anyway completely inaccurate was a turning point for Margaret Thatcher's attitude to the European Community. Until then she was prepared to seek compromises that would enable Britain to join common positions even when she was not convinced they were wholly in its interests. And that indeed remained the official policy of her government throughout the period. But in her mind, a Rubicon had been crossed. The pragmatism of her earlier years as Prime Minister gave way to a conviction that any further integration was no longer compatible with our sovereign statehood. Either Europe would have to change direction and slow down progress towards integration or Britain would increasingly distance itself from common European positions, as it already had over the Schengen Treaty, and stand aside from common positions on policies like the European Economic and Monetary Union (EMU) and the single currency. The fact that this put her increasingly at odds with the majority of her own Cabinet did not dismay her, though it produced some spectacular falling out in particular over Geoffrey Howe and Nigel Lawson's unimplemented threat to resign if she would not agree to set a date for Britain to join the Exchange Rate Mechanism.

It was against this background of frustration with what she saw as the European Community's incessant power grabs at the expense of the governments and Parliaments of the individual European nation states that Margaret Thatcher delivered her Bruges speech in 1988. It is the fullest statement of her views on

Europe and the European Community that she ever gave and still bears reading. But it is far from being the Eurosceptic charter it was subsequently labelled. Thatcher declared that:

> Britain does not dream of some cosy isolated existence on the fringes of the European Community. Our destiny is in Europe as part of the Community … The Community is not an end in itself. Nor is it an institutional device to be constantly modified according to the dictates of some abstract intellectual concept … The European Community is a practical means by which Europe can ensure the future prosperity and security of its people … I want to see us work more closely on the things we can do better together than alone. Europe is stronger when we do. But working more closely together does not require power to be centralised in Brussels or decisions to be taken by an appointed bureaucracy … We have not successfully rolled back the frontiers of the state in Britain only to see them reimposed at a European level with a European super-state exercising a new dominance from Brussels.

I would say those few sentences better articulate the fundamentals of Margaret Thatcher's view of Europe than anything else she said. And they were bolstered by positive proposals in favour of open markets, a Europe open to enterprise, strong transatlantic relations and readiness to bring the East and central European countries into the European Community as they moved out from under the Soviet shadow.

Why did her views not get a better reception in Europe or

indeed in parts of the British government? They were hardly the words of a deep-rooted opponent of everything European. Perhaps part of the reason is simply that they were delivered by Margaret Thatcher, who had become a hate figure in some British and European circles. However, I believe that there were two substantial reasons.

First the speech was delivered too late: two or three years earlier with Europe further away from the irrevocable steps on monetary union and other forms of integration, her manifesto for Europe's future could have secured a better hearing and wider support. Why the delay? Fundamentally, because Margaret Thatcher was preoccupied with other – and to her mind bigger – issues. The invitation from the College of Europe in Bruges had been outstanding for a number of years and the Foreign Office argued it was an embarrassment that she, unlike other European leaders, had not taken it up: an object lesson in being careful what you wish for. Anyway it was a case of the opportunity creating the speech rather than the speech representing a long-planned strike at the heart of European theology.

Second, and more fundamental, I think the high priests of integrationist ideology genuinely feared the impact and appeal of her ideas. After all, here was a woman who had stood British politics on its head and transformed Britain. Was it unthinkable that she might succeed in doing something similar in Europe by halting the focus on institution-building and transferring it instead to practical policies to people's benefit? For me at least, and I believe Margaret Thatcher too, the reaction demonstrated that the European elite feared open debate about Europe's future that might threaten their plans. And the results of some of the subsequent referendums in several European countries on the Maastricht Treaty, and later on the treaty establishing a Constitution for Europe, shows why they had cause to be worried. Margaret Thatcher's doubts about Europe's future course were, in their eyes, disturbingly widely shared – not that it stopped them from going ahead.

From this point on, Margaret Thatcher's thinking moved ever more on to the models and formulae for keeping Britain in the European Community without our being full participants – variable geometry Europe, inner and outer circles, opt-outs, a bespoke membership and the like. She no longer regarded it as worthwhile even trying to find compromises when decisions to extend the European Community's powers were at stake, witness the notorious 'No! No! No!' to Delors's proposals to treat the European Parliament – or as she invariably insisted on describing it, the European Assembly – as the democratic body of the European Community, the Commission as the Executive and the Council of Ministers as the Senate. She had no qualms about being isolated in Europe and when asked by the media on leaving a European Council meeting how she felt about being isolated eleven to one, replied with rash bravado: 'Sorry for the other eleven.' True, she grudgingly agreed later that Britain should join the Exchange Rate Mechanism, predicting accurately it would be a disaster, but the reason was that she could not afford the resignation of a second Chancellor as well as a second Foreign Secretary over the issue. In the light of Brexit, it's ironic that her determination to prevent the European Community from encroaching too far on the powers of national governments and parliaments cost her the leadership of the Tory Party and her political career.

I will deal only briefly with Margaret Thatcher's post-No. 10 views on Europe. Freed from the constraints of government, she became steadily more critical of the Community. She demonstrated scant loyalty to her successor's attempts to battle with the same issues she had, affirming that she could never have signed up to Maastricht, but would have opposed it root and branch, overlooking John Major's success in negotiating opt-outs, which was the very course on which she herself was set.

Even in retirement, she never categorically proposed that Britain should leave the (by then) European Union, though she certainly discussed the possibility. She wrote wistfully that by rejecting de Gaulle's proposal for association between Britain and the EEC, following the breakdown of negotiations in 1964, 'we missed the best European bus that ever came along'. What I can say with confidence is that she never discussed or pursued the option of leaving while she was Prime Minister. She was scathing about the futility of empty-chair policies as practised by the Soviet Union at the UN and President de Gaulle in Europe. And she detested referendums, describing them as instruments of tyranny. Her efforts were directed instead to changing the European Community not to abandoning it, and over a decade after leaving office she was still asserting that 'our destiny is in Europe'. The more doctrinaire Eurosceptics will point out that she said 'Europe' not the 'European Community'. But Margaret Thatcher was not one to make self-evident assertions.

So how does Margaret Thatcher's record look? I will suggest seven distinct conclusions.

First, stand back and look at her premiership as a whole. She wrought extraordinary changes in our country, rebuilt its international standing and contributed mightily to the single most far-reaching change in the world scene in the second half of the twentieth century with the end of the Cold War. Her policies on Europe had a role in that, but much more in terms of defence and security than of the European Community. No one could credibly say that the European Community was a sideshow, but its activities contributed less to the collapse of the Soviet Union and global communism than did NATO or the efforts of the key individual member states: the UK, Germany and France.

Margaret Thatcher herself was focused on the liberation of central and Eastern Europe while Brussels was still in the grip of old-style Ostpolitik. So when judging her overall record as Prime Minister, one needs to keep the relative importance of her opposition to ever closer European integration in proportion.

Second, she undoubtedly did get some things wrong about Europe. She never understood the deep emotions that building the European Community and later the Union aroused in Continental Europe. She was mistaken to think that expressions like 'political union' meant less than the words and to insist that since no one could define it, it must be meaningless. She could not take idealistic rhetoric seriously and as a result underestimated how much it would guide the actual policies of other Europeans. For her, the European Community was basically a trading framework and a useful vehicle for foreign policy co-operation, not a vision of Europe's future.

Third, while she may have made mistakes, she made some very sound judgements too. She disliked the European Community's constant resort to new institution-building rather than substantive policy solutions whenever faced with a problem. She regarded its attachment to the value of state intervention in the economy as yesterday's future. She never bought into the concept that only by being part of a bigger unit could Britain promote its interests in the future. In her eyes, the advantages of size could be achieved by like-minded allies working together rather than requiring integration. And anyway, she believed that the will to act and having the right ideas and instincts were a lot more important to global influence than size.

Fourth, whatever the rights and wrongs of her views, she did an astonishing job for Britain from getting our money back, to implementing the single market, to preparing the way for East European countries to enter the Community, to keeping us out of the Schengen Agreement, to a host of more detailed gains. Her main aim throughout was to make our membership of the European Community good for Britain even if that meant not always behaving as a 'good European'. Other countries were no less determined to extract national advantage from the EC, but were better at concealing it beneath a mass of idealistic verbiage.

Fifth, would she have served Britain's national interest better by being less forceful, less outspoken, less shrill, by acting as a better European and by being readier to accept compromises? That seemed to be the view of quite a large part of her own government. I disagree. The gains we made could only have been achieved by a tough, no-holds-barred negotiator prepared to ignore every attempt to intimidate her. Neither the patronising put-downs of President Giscard d'Estaing and Chancellor Schmidt, nor the bluster of Chancellor Kohl, nor the sulks of President Delors put her off from securing what Britain needed and deserved. Would a more communautaire approach have secured us even more? It may have made us more likeable but I see no evidence that our concrete interests would have been better served. I developed a habit of slipping into European heads of government meetings in the late afternoon, when I sensed Margaret Thatcher might be flagging, taking her a whisky. Chancellor Kohl once beckoned me over when he was in the chair and begged me not to do it: 'You are making her worse,' he said. 'That's the whole point, Herr Bundeskanzler,' I replied.

Sixth, could Margaret Thatcher have done more to heal the divisions over Europe in her own party? It's hard to see how. The existence of a hard core of Eurosceptics in the Conservative Party predated her time as Prime Minister. She met regularly with them to explain and justify the government's policies, and they could hardly have accused her of failing in her duty to stand up vigorously for British interests in Europe and fight against European policies that were inimical to the free market philosophy of the government. But there were limits to how far she was prepared to be influenced by Eurosceptics. The Bruges Speech was not a surrender to them but a manifesto for a new direction for Europe that would make the European Community more successful, not undermine and weaken Britain's membership.

Margaret Thatcher as Prime Minister fought for a better Europe that would be more in tune with the requirements of economic prosperity and international security. Her battle was not to emasculate it, let alone abandon it.

Last, did Margaret Thatcher's intransigence in Europe make eventual Brexit inevitable? Britain was the 'awkward' squad for other Europeans long before Margaret Thatcher took an interest in European affairs and remained so after she stepped down. In reality, there has been an incompatible tension between inter-governmentalism and integrationism at the heart of Britain's membership of the EU from the beginning. The Heath government that took Britain into Europe glossed over that fundamental divide. Even so, the tension was successfully managed for many years, making EU membership on balance a good enough deal for the UK to tolerate the constraints which it imposed and to keep the country united on our continued membership. The fact that it became unmanageable in 2016 was as much down to political mishandling as to ineluctable historical forces: mistakes such as Tony Blair's pushing Britain further towards integration than was acceptable to the middle ground of British politics, and David Cameron's belief that a referendum would draw the poison of Europe which had by then so infected the Conservative Party. And the mistakes of handling were as much on the European side as the British one. I find it hard to believe that Chancellor Kohl and President Mitterrand would have refused Margaret Thatcher an emergency brake on immigration.

Margaret Thatcher's aim was to secure Britain's essential interests within the European Community while protecting us from outcomes which would have irretrievably jeopardised our nationhood, our parliamentary sovereignty and our right to govern ourselves. She did so in a way that saved us from having to face the choice between staying and leaving, in her time at least. Her successors, both in Britain and in Europe, have been less successful – and are likely to regret it.

CHAPTER 10

JOHN MAJOR

CHRIS PATTEN

'It is in the interests of Britain ... to be part of the development of our continent. By part I do not mean a walk-on part; I do not mean simply being a member. I mean playing a leading role in the European Community.'

JOHN MAJOR, HOUSE OF COMMONS, SEPTEMBER 1992

The metaphors multiply, ransacking a whole lexicon of modes of transport. The British express train with tabloid editors heaving coals into the fire chamber, rough rides across the sleepers – clickety-click – towards a violent crash. The car with the Conservative Party in the back seat (who knows who is in the front?) speeds increasingly out of control towards a fork in the road. The Not-so-Easyjet takes off, with no one at ground control able to tell the pilot where or when he is to land. Or perhaps instead of all this 'enemies of the people' stuff, the ship of state, liberated at last, weighs anchor and sets course, the wind of freedom in its sails, for the open seas and distant horizons. Take your pick.

Well, I took mine years ago: an 'enemy of the people,' guilty as charged. I guess this affects whatever I say about John Major and the impact of the European debate on his seven-year premiership during the course of which the roots of today's problems were dug in and watered.

There is another confession that I must make. John is a friend, the ablest member of my political generation in the Conservative Party, the cleverest of the three party leaders for whom I worked, and one of the most decent people to lead both country and party for years. His premiership was both undermined and attenuated by arguments about Europe, the source and the consequences of which I will try to describe in this chapter without plodding from one European Council meeting to another.

It is stretching vocabulary to describe this story as a tragedy. There is nothing resembling the Oresteia about it – blood only occasionally stains the carpet. Nor is there the sort of history-shaking drama of Suez, when a clever, vain and ill Prime Minister reran history and discovered in the course of doing so the new reality of Britain's role in the world – a middle-ranking power whose future as a great nation was threatened by its delusion that it was still a great power. It is this same abuse of history that was part of the problem facing John, and it has morphed into today's national psycho-drama.

Let's begin with the history. Our deliberate choice – despite the hope of our best friend across the Atlantic – not to take part in the creation of what was to become the European Union has dogged our subsequent membership. Some years after we declined to be one of the founding fathers, having failed to find an alternative to common market membership in the European Free Trade Association (EFTA), we concluded that we should no longer exclude ourselves from a historic European cooperation in which some notional de jure sovereignty was traded in for greater de facto sovereignty.

For France and Germany, who were at the heart of this creation, the case for a historic reconciliation was a 'no-brainer'. France achieved what the bloodshed and humiliation of two wars had not accomplished: a peaceful settlement with its biggest neighbour and competitor – the Sparta to its Athens. No longer would armies fight across Alsace-Lorraine; instead diplomats would argue deep into the night in debating chambers in Strasbourg, where French negotiators were able to secure arrangements that heavily subsidised rural France and tied German industry into Europe's common market.

For Germany, the Messina agreement offered an exit from half a century of calamitous history in which, to borrow from Auden:

In the nightmare of the dark
All the dogs of Europe bark.

Germany had barked loudest and suffered most, reduced by wicked excess to moral, economic and political rubble. The creation of a structure to unite Western Europe offered Germany the chance to bury the past in an institutionalised reaffirmation of the values and civilisation to which Germany had contributed so much in the past. Into the bargain, this would also make the rest of Europe feel safe with Germany as friend not enemy.

What of Britain – the third of Europe's most significant makers and shapers? Where was the narrative that would underpin our relationship with Europe? When we tried to create one we often stumbled over the task, with our characteristic insistence on the practical and the pragmatic over starry-eyed visions. For some who had fought in one or other of the world wars the argument for membership was overwhelmingly obvious, and moral too. Macmillan bore the scar of the five wounds he had suffered fighting in the First World War. He had lost many of the friends with whom at Oxford he had studied the classic texts of Western culture. Ted Heath and Roy Jenkins in their turn had grown up through the years of rampant fascism and had fought in another European civil war. Yet all of them, try as they might (and Jenkins especially did it explicitly and well) found it hard to shake off the national self-delusion of Britain's post-war place in the world.

Churchill articulated better than any others the case for a different way of governing what he called 'the noble Continent'. He also accepted, in his own words, the need 'to part with a degree of national sovereignty … for the sake of a larger synthesis … national sovereignty is not inviolable, and … may be resolutely diminished for the sake of all men in all the lands finding their way home together'.

After Maastricht and the ejection from the ERM, John Major made the same argument very clearly in the House of Commons reflecting the needs at the end of the century:

> It is in the interests of Britain – our interests, our objectives and our prosperity – for us to be part of the development of our continent. By part I do not mean a walk-on part; I do not mean simply being a member. I mean playing a leading role in the European Community. I mean helping to determine the direction of policy, building the policies that we want and fighting those that we do not want. We will need to compromise on some matters, but so will every national state in Europe unless we return to tribalism right across the European Community.

In his view, Britain clearly still had a place in helping Europeans to '[find] their way home together'.

So, he argued elsewhere, to surprising consternation on the Conservative right, that we should be 'at the heart of Europe'.

John and I were part of a generation, the first of our century, that had not fought in a war or been prepared to do so through military conscription. We were well aware of Britain's heroic exploits during the Second World War – of standing alone, of bearing great costs in blood and treasure in the name of freedom, our own and that of other nations. But we were also aware, to put this point a little too directly for some, that that was then. We have become, as the years have slipped past, a diminished country politically and economically, not unimportant, not second-rate, but no longer the power we once were. There was no empire, and we were no longer one of the world's major workshops. We had been diminished partly because of the rise of others, first in Europe, then in Asia, partly by our own mistakes, and partly by the ineluctable and welcome progress of others.

We could not continue to strut our stuff as the then independent point of balance between Europe, the United States and the Commonwealth; to use Churchill's words, the sole member of these three rings: the Lord of the Rings as it were. We could not simply go our own way, respected by others, bankrolled by others because of what we had once been. We had to earn respect for what we were and could become, a middle-sized, pretty fair and tolerant country that could influence and even lead its neighbours, but that could not go it alone without costs to our own well-being, influence and prestige. You could sing 'Jerusalem' until you were blue in the face (with its first verse of questions to all of which incidentally the answer is a negative); but however loudly we sang it, it was not enough to bring home the bacon and to overcome the challenges of the late twentieth century and beyond.

John was not a great linguist; no more am I. But he knew enough about our continent and its history to recognise three things. First, culturally, politically, economically and genetically our history was tangled with that of our neighbours. How could it not be, given that all that separated us from our continent was a few miles of cold sea water? Our language and our law made by precedent could admittedly claim a relatively self-contained history at least for almost a millennium. Yet some of our greatest monarchs had come from foreign stock. We were, to borrow from Daniel Defoe, a 'mongrel breed'. We had been launched on our greatest century of liberty and prosperity by a Dutchman. Moreover, invariably when we had isolated ourselves from our neighbours, there was trouble. We provided an important balance in an occasionally turbulent continent. Naturally, therefore, Major sought to develop as strong a relationship as possible with the leaders of France and Germany.

So far as 'l'Hexagone' was concerned, there can have been few personalities more different from Major than former President Mitterrand, the emperor of ambivalence, who slipped out of one skin into another with neither embarrassment nor much by way of integrity. No *tu* or *-toi* there, he lapped up flattery, requiring, as Helmet Kohl said, that when meeting him you should first bow three times to the tricolour.

Switching countries, I can personally attest to the warmth of Major's relationship, actually friendship, with Helmut Kohl. The great German, an initially underestimated leader, warmed to Major and took him seriously as a like-minded conservative with a social conscience. A good relationship is not always better than a transactional approach to international affairs. People can love you to bits in a meeting, but shaft you when it suits them. We almost certainly exaggerated how much Kohl would help us to manage our fraught position in the ERM in 1992. If Kohl had to choose between a row with the Bundesbank or a row with Britain, you did not need to be a genius to know who he would support. Yet, overall, relationships do matter and they can assist a lot at the margins, helping you in European negotiations for example to get your own way in the darkest passages of the night. Relationships attract goodwill; they afford you the benefit of the doubt rather than the reverse.

Major was brilliant at this, as he showed at Maastricht, partly because he recognised that, like him, others had to deal with political pressures at home, partly because he was a naturally gifted negotiator, always knowing his brief better than anyone else knew their own, and partly because of his transparent decency. I doubt whether many who dealt with him disliked him, though they probably sympathised with him in part because of his predecessor and the party he had to attempt to lead.

This was and remains today a central part of the European story. Jock Bruce-Gardyne, a forward-thinking, clever, right-wing Eurosceptic MP, is said to have remarked about Margaret Thatcher that she had saved Britain but would destroy the Conservative Party. Both deserved their fate, he concluded. These propositions are exaggerated, but there is some truth in his assertions. I fear that some Conservatives seem intent on making the second come true.

John Major's European inheritance from Thatcher was mixed. She had swung her handbag to good effect to get a fairer budgetary settlement for Britain than the one that followed inevitably from the arrangements made before we became members. She had driven through the creation of the single market, sustained by the Single European Act and the extension of qualified majority voting. She had been insistent on standing up for economic and political freedom in the centre and east of the Continent, among the countries of the Warsaw Pact. All this was admirable, yet I doubt that it was necessary to offend all her interlocutors quite so much in order to accomplish these considerable successes.

Margaret Thatcher in government was of course always more sensible and cautious than she was after her defenestration, arguably an act that would have been better left to the country than carried out by her party. (It did not, however, feel like that at the time). In retirement, her good sense was overwhelmed by often ill-informed prejudice. I was once privileged to hear, admittedly late at night when the whole company was enjoying 'the lovely stuff' (as Anne Fleming called alcohol), Margaret's pocket history of Europe. France and Germany did not emerge well from her account; it would have seemed like a caricature even in the intemperate hands of a tabloid editorial writer. We know of course that she attempted – an embarrassing failure – to foil the reunification of Germany.

Margaret Thatcher was probably led on by acolytes, who told her that her principled stand against turning Europe into a federal state (not something that was ever likely to happen) was the reason why she lost office. Maybe they had never heard of the poll tax. In any event, they encouraged her, and she encouraged them, in mutually reinforcing serial acts of disloyalty to her successor. That disloyalty was vigorously encouraged by Norman Tebbit, who had once chivvied and bullied his parliamentary colleagues into supporting the Single European Act.

Reading John Major's memoirs, it is remarkable how restrained he is in describing what he called 'a pathological source of division within the Conservative Party'. Explaining on one occasion to Stephen Wall – perhaps his principal adviser on Europe and one of several clever and sensible Foreign Office diplomats who tilled this stony ground over the years – why he could not be bolder on some aspect or other of EU policy, he said, 'You forget that I am standing astride a crack in the Conservative Party that is growing wider by the day.'

This would have amazed me when I made my mostly involuntary departure from domestic British politics in 1992. We had after all just won an election in which Europe had hardly been mentioned save in the context of John Major's diplomatic triumph at Maastricht. It was certainly a mistake to be quite so enthusiastic at the conclusion of this council meeting about what had been achieved – 'game, set and match'. This was, however, a pretty accurate assessment of the outcome. A close friend of mine who was at Maastricht as Europe minister, Tristan Garel-Jones, when discussing his territorial designation on becoming a member of the House of Lords, asked if he could choose Maastricht. 'We are sorry,' he was told, 'but normally one can only choose a foreign place if it was the scene of a great British victory.' Precisely, Tristan replied, though he had to settle for Watford.

At Maastricht, Major got everything Britain wanted and it underpinned the extent to which we achieved membership of the European Union on the terms that best suited us. We had the single market and enlargement without the Social Chapter and any commitment to signing up to monetary union. We were in due course to secure opt-outs from the Schengen Agreement in the Amsterdam Treaty during the Blair premiership.

So in the early summer of 1992, why should anyone have predicted the growing turbulence over Europe which has deeply troubled the Conservative Party to the present day and has made it ever more difficult for party leaders to pursue what most have believed to be the national interest, while keeping the Conservative Party together?

John Major's account of what happened is remarkably free of rancour. The relatively small parliamentary majority secured by the Conservative Party in 1992, in comparison with its plurality of votes, made party rebellion particularly destabilising, even more so since the Labour opposition chose to support Conservative rebellions rather than focus on their view of Britain's European role. Legislation to implement Maastricht had been postponed, fatally it transpired, until after the election. One of the main reasons this decision was made was undoubtedly the positive reception initially given to the outcome of the treaty negotiations. The passage of the legislation itself was bedevilled by Black Wednesday (the ejection from the ERM), the 'no' vote in the Danish referendum and anxieties about the outcome of the French referendum. A group of backbenchers, several of them new to Parliament, emboldened by Margaret Thatcher's 'Queen over the water' much-denied plotting and by an increasingly hostile press, demonstrated day after day, week after week, the fiction of the proposition that loyalty is the Conservative Party's secret weapon.

Attempts through compromise to curtail rebellions got nowhere. Major promoted opponents; the 'bastards' became even bigger bastards as they got their hands on a red box. He blocked the nomination of the Belgian Jean-Luc Dehaene as President of the Commission and got in his place a less wily and more federalist Luxembourger. We conceded a referendum on potential membership of EMU. Our able Foreign Secretary, Malcolm Rifkind, was sent around Europe to lecture other states on the sort of union they really wanted if only they realised. Our negotiators were periodically obliged to tie themselves in knots over voting rights and enlargement. Over an issue where most people around the negotiating table behaved badly – BSE in British herds – we seemed to go along with the tabloid depiction of the argument as a European assault – on the sanctity of roast beef as our national culinary story. None of these political gestures made a scrap of difference to the Europhobes, which would not have surprised Rudyard Kipling:

> But we've proved it again and again,
> That if once you have paid him the Dane-geld
> You never get rid of the Dane.

I assume that Major has compared notes on Danegeld with David Cameron and Theresa May.

What can you do if some in your party put dogma before evidence, ideology before country; or if they are prepared to make their party increasingly unelectable at a time when the majority of their parliamentary colleagues still wish to continue working for what they believe is the national interest? And the story is not yet over.

In his memoirs, Major asks – without any sign of self-pity – 'Was there something I could have said, some policy I could have adopted, someone I should have fired, someone I could have hired, a speech, a broadcast, an argument which might have begun my party's journey back to sanity?' He goes on to ask rhetorically, 'Could a different man have done it?' Neither a man nor a woman, we now know could have done it. If a party is hell-bent on self-destruction there is not much you can do about it, so it appears. The biggest problem (looking beyond partisan politics) is the collateral damage to the country, both externally and at home.

So, 'stuff happens,' as former US Secretary of Defense Donald Rumsfeld used to say. Was all the recent trouble caused by John Major's views on Europe, by – for example – a departure from the sacred texts of Thatcherism? When anyone actually describes John Major's idea of how Europe should best work, and how Britain should conduct itself within the Union, you rapidly become aware of a description that sounds boringly platitudinous. He spelt out what he describes as the result of his musings on holiday one summer in the Douro Valley (presumably spurred on by the then Ambassador to Portugal, Stephen Wall), in an article for the Economist in 1995.

'It is for nations,' he wrote,

> to build Europe, not for Europe to attempt to supersede nations. I want to see the Community become a wide union, embracing the whole of democratic Europe, in a single market and with common security arrangements firmly linked to NATO. I want to see a competitive and confident Europe, generating jobs for its citizens and choice for its consumers. A Community which ceases to nibble at national freedoms, and so commands the enthusiasm of its member states.

And he continued, such a community would offer peace, security, more free trade and safeguards for infant democracies. It would reflect 'the instincts of free people in the nations' and retune the Treaty of Rome to make it more relevant for the times.

The exposition of this thoroughly sensible objective did not immediately lead to unilateral disarmament of those within

Europe who had federalist ambitions with which Britain would not go along and which remained a distant dream. Yet 'ever closer union' has always meant, and is likely always to mean 'ever closer union among freely cooperating sovereign governments' (to borrow the phrase from Major's successor). Did Major ever do anything that could raise suspicions that he was intent on another destination? You certainly could not say that about the Exchange Rate Mechanism, entered in weakness while Thatcher was in Downing Street, and left in humiliation. The consequences of the illusory Lawson boom in the late 1980s persuaded most British policy makers, including the then Prime Minister, that it provided our best chance of cutting interest rates while stabilising the exchange rate, enabling us to promote growth and job creation without stoking inflation.

Our unceremonious exit was the consequence of several factors. First, politics was starting to have an unsettling effect on the financial markets. The Danes had voted to reject the Maastricht Treaty, and France had just announced that they would hold a referendum on the treaty as well. Second, and more important, the costs of German reunification had pushed the Bundesbank into a tougher monetary stance. Higher interest rates there were attracting a great tide of money from Wall Street as the US dollar weakened. A stronger Deutsche Mark and high German interest rates put a huge strain on other currencies in the ERM, above all sterling, the lira and the franc.

Major's experience of trying to cope with membership of the Exchange Rate Mechanism did nothing to dilute his existing opposition to Britain joining the monetary union. He foresaw all the problems of a monetary union embracing countries of widely varying economic performance. How could such an arrangement be sustained without fiscal and political union, with stronger economies needing to make substantial transfers to weaker ones. Germany and Greece spring quickly to mind. He had seen the merits of a common but not a single currency; a common currency based on a strong euro driving out of use over time weaker currencies. In retrospect this looks like a very much better idea than EMU. Had as much political effort in Europe gone into another cause, like completion of the single market, as has gone into holding the Eurozone together, our Continental economy would have been even stronger, though it does now seem to be emerging from its long-running and flatlining difficulties.

What Major did here and elsewhere was to preserve Britain from being 'shackled to a corpse', to borrow from the vocabulary of Brexiteers. These days the corpse seems to have enjoyed a Lazarus-like emergence from the tomb, with the funeral party now looking in a different direction west from Picardy. But the most important point is this: Major helped us to get membership of the EU on the terms which we thought best suited us. We grumbled about the Welfare Bills in Continental Europe holding back economic growth – but our welfare state was almost certainly less generous and expensive than that in our major competitor countries. We grumbled about an excessively regulated labour market – but according to the OECD we had the least regulated market in the EU. We criticised the EMU – but we were not part of it. We pointed to Europe's demographic challenges – but free movement of people in Europe had added brain and muscle power to our workforce. Now that Polish plumbers are going home, who will deal with the leaks in the kitchen? Perhaps our old age pensioners will have the time to do it, in between – as leading Brexiteers have suggested – picking peas in Lincolnshire or digging for Britain.

So Major's stewardship of our European Union membership, while not perfect, did underpin the fact that we were members of a Union, which we had done so much to create, along the lines that we wanted. We negotiated a membership which suited us. What's not to like, as they say?

What's not to like, apparently, is that the price for all this was that we had lost much of our sovereignty. We had not just stood by and watched as nefarious foreigners carried off great chunks of it, as though it had been hacked from the Cenotaph. We had actually helped to transport all these vandalised pieces to Brussels and Strasbourg.

Sovereignty is not nothing. There are clearly limits to it in terms of the area over which you believe it extends: a government's sovereignty does not normally extend beyond its borders. It can grow and diminish according to external and internal circumstances; it is not like virginity, as Geoffrey Howe used to say, here one moment and gone the next. Yet plainly you do need to know at any one time where it is located. And in Britain there has always been one answer. It rests legally, de jure, with Parliament in Westminster. If Parliament wishes, it can decline to pool any of its sovereignty with others – NATO, the WTO or the EU for example. We are at present intent on reversing the pooling of sovereignty to which we freely agreed. We are doing this because of a departure from what we have always believed in the past to be our preferred method of accountability, decisions taken in Parliament. The referendum rules, OK? Not if you were Edmund Burke. Not if you were Margaret Thatcher. And why are we to do it? Because we believe that we 'must take back control' of our destiny, take back control in a world where most of the problems faced by individual member states, including let it be said mass immigration, can only be dealt with through international cooperation.

How had we lost control of our ability to run our education system (not conspicuously well), or our health service, or our welfare service, or our steadily diminishing defence forces? The main area where we had allegedly lost control was in the creation of a genuine single market. As Margaret Thatcher said, 'Almost every major nation has been obliged by the pressure of the post-war world to pool significant areas of sovereignty so as to create more effective political units.' That is why we agreed in the Single European Act to give away allegedly hunks of our parliamentary sovereignty. Who were the enemies of the people when the Single European Act was being whipped through Parliament?

Now, while sovereignty is a notoriously slippery idea, slithering down the slope from the divine right of kings and the will of God to the will of the people, there are limits which most of us would put on the distance and duration of the slide. This was true for John Major, who, unlike some of his political colleagues, wished to stop the slide in about the same position as the passing of time suggests is sensible. He did not believe that monetary union was possible without political union. He reckoned that this would raise far more profound issues of sovereignty that would be difficult to sell to electorates in their own countries. So what has changed? President Macron, whom I much admire, was in his early teens when the Conservative Party was racked by all these rows in the 1990s. Perhaps the hand on the clock has moved far more rapidly than I think is the case. Perhaps we have arrived already at a day in the twenty-first century when a German Finance minister will be able to decide the rate of VAT on French restaurant bills. Perhaps… I suspect that Madame Le Pen will not be the only person in France to tell the clever President that such a destination is not '*vaut le voyage*'.

Meanwhile with admiration and mild alarm, we will watch the French President's efforts to increase the margin between French and British productivity by even more than the existing 20 per cent. But I forgot, our abysmal and steadily impoverishing rate of productivity must be a result of our membership of the EU, mustn't it? Take back control and all will be well. Get rid of the EU and watch British productivity soar.

De facto and de jure sovereignty – reality and delusion. Remember Shakespeare's *Henry IV Part I*:

> Glendower: 'I can call spirits from the vasty deep.'
> Hotspur: 'Why so can I, or so can any man;
> But will they come when you do call for them?

Well, the spirits are summoned. Boris Johnson and the tabloid editors are on the case. And, forget not, if they don't arrive on time by March 2019 we will be to blame.

Which brings me to my final point. An important chorus in the drama of John's negotiations with Brussels and with the Conservative Party was the media, more specifically the British media, parts of which have been the catalysts in moulding opinion on Europe over the years, and whose role will be even more significant and divisive I fear over the coming months and years. Given their activities during the Major premiership, I have always been surprised that he was not more critical of them. In his memoirs, he does refer to the 'tweedy fantasies' of some of the pretentious fogeys who patronised and ridiculed him. He noted how often 'fantasies … took the place of facts'. He talks about all this '[ripping] into my premiership, [damaging] the Conservative Party and [coming] close to destroying the government.' I think it often hurt him; it would have hurt me. It certainly hurt the Conservative Party and will, as like as not, help bring the Conservative Party to the verge of breaking point and the country to a period of divisive bitterness. Indeed, it has come close to doing that already.

Shaped as we are by the Enlightenment and its values, we should defend free speech and a free press. We may not like journalists or newspapers with whose opinions we disagree, but toleration of them is part of the wholly acceptable price of living in a democracy that is pluralist and free. The best response to bad free speech is good free speech. I gave evidence to the Leveson Inquiry arguing against greater parliamentary or government regulation of the press. In doing so I often wondered why it was that trust in our public service broadcaster was so very much – indeed, mountainously – higher than that in our newspapers, despite the regular assaults that some of them made on its journalistic integrity.

All of which is a prequel to that most commanding of all conjunctions. What should we think about newspapers that show little regard for the truth, which promote their own divisive agenda, which whip up hate against those with a different view of Britain's best interests? What should we feel about newspapers who regard those with whom they disagree as unpatriotic enemies? Isn't all this worth debating without fear of the next day's hatchet headline?

The end of this European drama may well be our departure from the Union. We may 'take back control', wherever it is that control resides. I hope such 'control' includes promoting the civility of public discourse. I trust we will not lose the civic culpability that has been such a hallmark of our public life at its regular best. I fear losing this even more than I worry about the consequence, economic and political, of departing the EU. I think that Major was an example, despite the squalls and storms, of the attempt to hold on to that value while leading a divided party and attempting to do what he thought best for the country. And what next? To return once more to William Shakespeare, as King John says to a messenger bringing ill tidings, 'So foul a sky clears not without a storm.' I hope that in Britain the storm does not blow away too much of what really matters to this civilised country.

CHAPTER 11

TONY BLAIR

ANDREW ADONIS

'Tony Blair, Cherie Booth QC, Rupert Murdoch, Alastair Campbell. Lunch, 3 May 1997.'

FIRST ENTRY IN THE VISITORS BOOK IN CHEQUERS AFTER TONY BLAIR'S ELECTION VICTORY

In my diaries there is this wonderful story Tony Blair told of President Chirac:

> Jacques told me how surprised he was that we had a homosexual in the Cabinet. He'd been reading about Chris Smith. 'We couldn't possibly do that in France,' he said. 'Oh,' I said, 'I've got four in my Cabinet.' His jaw dropped. 'Four? Four?' he repeated. 'Mon Dieu, dear Tony, and you can't even join the euro!'

Advancing gay rights was one of Tony Blair's great achievements.

By contrast, his support for the euro never came out of the closet and his greatest legacy on Europe is something which at the time of enlargement in 2004 he said would never happen: the migration to Britain of one and a half million Poles and other central and Eastern Europeans, which is one of the reasons why we may be leaving the European Union.

My diaries contain two contemporary notes by Tony on his legacy written shortly before he left office in June 2007. In the first, he writes of 'A nation open, at ease with globalisation, prepared to compete on its merits not its history.' Of Britain's international standing, he says, 'We took Britain's key alliances, Europe and America, and kept them both strong. In Europe, the UK went from the Beef War and isolation to leading the debates on European defence, economic reform, energy, enlargement, and did the Budget deal.' In another note, he is more succinct: 'On Europe, we have moved from the sidelines to the Centre. We have been prepared to defy Eurosceptic opinion to do so.'

Ten years on, we aren't just on the sidelines, we are leaving the stadium; and the Eurosceptics are running the country.

Both mine and Tony's great friend and mentor Roy Jenkins once likened Tony's attitude to power to the museum curator carrying a priceless Ming vase across a slippery floor, desperate not to drop it. The European vase is now on the floor, in a thousand pieces. David Cameron dropped it, but the inescapable question for this chapter is: what role did Tony play in polishing the floor? And what are the lessons of the Blair decade?

Tony was the most instinctively pro-European Prime Minister since Edward Heath. Indeed, he had two big advantages over

Heath: he was a member of the human race – and he enjoyed meeting people, including foreigners, not least the French.

Tony spoke colloquial French, learnt in a Paris bar as a student, which he deployed before the Assemblée Nationale to admiration. He took most of his holidays in the south of France or Tuscany. By my calculation, he spent in total more than half a year on holiday in France or Italy during his decade as Prime Minister, more than any Prime Minister since Lord Salisbury, who had a château near Dieppe.

I still recall the tense office discussion after the 2001 foot and mouth crisis on whether, just for once, the Prime Minister might take a holiday in the country he ruled, to show solidarity. He wasn't – how shall I put it – at all keen on this idea. The best Anji Hunter and Sally Morgan could extract was two days in Cornwall, which he and Cherie enjoyed only marginally more than their annual visit to Balmoral with the Royal Family. It rained solidly, and they were on the next Ryanair to Carcassonne.

When Tony says in his memoirs, 'I regarded anti-European feeling as hopelessly, absurdly out of date and unrealistic,' this is from the heart and soul. He could and still does express his Europeanism with extraordinary passion – as when he received the Charlemagne Prize in Aachen Cathedral in 1999 – and it is part of the reason why so many of us admire him so much.

Tony had another advantage: a united pro-European party. John Major had been torn limb from limb by right-wing Eurosceptics he called 'bastards'. By the 1990s, there were few overt Eurosceptics in the Labour Party, and none in the leadership, thanks to the Social Chapter and the seminal speech by Jacques

Delors to the TUC conference in 1988 – a speech that Charles Powell, in his chapter on Margaret Thatcher, identified as the turning point in her attitude to the EU.

I now realise how significant was the fact that the Bruges speech, drafted by Charles, came precisely twelve days after Jacques Delors' appearance in Bournemouth. Thatcher was deliberately replying to Delors, just as the very title of Delors's speech, 'The Social Dimension of Europe', had been designed to enrage her. Hence the oddity that contemporary Euroscepticism was born in Bruges and Labour pro-Europeanism in Bournemouth.

So the New Labour new dawn, which rose over Britain – or at least the Royal Festival Hall – on 2 May 1997, appeared to herald a rebirth of Europe too. However, in retrospect, there were storm clouds even as the sun rose.

First, New Labour normalised referendums and opened the way to anti-European populism. At the time we thought referendums were a good idea. I wrote a Demos pamphlet with Geoff Mulgan entitled 'Back to Greece: the case for Direct Democracy'. It was full of juvenile, simplistic arguments of which I am now ashamed.

Before 1997 there had been only one national referendum and two other referendums (in Scotland and Wales) in mainland Britain, all within the space of four years in the turbulent, ungovernable 1970s.

The argument could be made – and was made – that the 1975 referendum on the European Community and the 1979 referendums on devolution to Scotland and Wales were aberrations caused by government and party breakdown, not democratic principle. Charles Powell writes above that Mrs Thatcher 'detested' referendums. She never held one; nor did John Major, even in the darkest days of Maastricht.

Then New Labour came along and held five referendums, two almost immediately after the 1997 election, finally clinching Scottish and Welsh devolution, followed by three more in the next decade. Faced with the not particularly controversial question of giving the proposed Scottish Parliament modest tax-raising powers, Tony imposed a second question in the Scottish devolution referendum in order to avoid an argument with the Tories and the right-wing media on higher taxes north of the border. Later there were referendums on the London mayoralty and a regional assembly for the north-east – essentially matters of local government reorganisation – and even on a proposal for a congestion charge in Manchester.

After all this referendumitis, it was going to be hard to avoid an in/out referendum on Europe at some point, particularly with the 1975 precedent, the regular referendums in the rest of the EU, and the rise of UKIP, a party which grew out of the Referendum Party, whose sole policy was an in/out referendum on the EU.

Tony led a long way towards this by coming out for a referendum on membership of the euro as one of his first acts of leadership in 1994. Then, in 2005, he declared for a referendum on former French President Giscard d'Estaing's proposed European Constitution.

Herein lies another Chirac tale. Chirac was under pressure to grant a referendum on the European Constitution. Once Tony had unexpectedly come out for one, Chirac felt he had to follow, despite Gerhard Schröder's opposition. The French referendum was held before the British. It was lost by a decisive fifty-five to forty-five margin, whereupon the constitution was repackaged as the Lisbon Treaty. Tony argued that Lisbon didn't require a referendum because it was a treaty not a constitution – let's not dwell on that distinction – and he got away with it because everyone knew that if there was a referendum on Lisbon, it would have been lost.

Tony's comment in his memoirs about this lucky escape takes on a greater significance in retrospect.

> As ever, I was sanguine. I thought we might just turn it into a referendum that was effectively: in or out … My advisers disagreed, but I rather fancied mounting a really big public argument on an issue I felt strongly about and on which I was right. I could also see how, in the course of such a campaign, the progressive alliance – fractured over Iraq – might heal. So although plainly a tough challenge, I somewhat relished the fight.

To which one can only reply: mon Dieu.

Anyway, it was a short step from all this referendumitis to the Cameron–Clegg coalition's national referendum on electoral reform in 2011; its eleven referendums on directly elected mayors in English cities a year later; its legislation mandating referendums for all new EU treaties; the Lib Dems and then David Cameron coming out for an in/out referendum; and finally the cataclysm of 23 June 2016.

This second storm cloud on the horizon on 2 May 1997 was Tony's attitude to the euro.

From the moment the 1992 Maastricht Treaty gave Britain

an opt-in to the single currency – into the planning of it before 1999 and directly into the currency after its launch in 1999 – the question of whether or not to join had to be answered. It was the key unavoidable question facing the British state in the run-up to the 1997 election and for the entirety of the Blair government.

In immediate economic terms it wasn't obvious, then or now, where British interests lay. Put five economists in a room in the 1990s and you got six answers – unless one of them was my friend Ed Balls, when the other four fled with mortal injuries.

This is still the case today. Preparing for this essay I asked four distinguished economists whether the euro would survive and whether, if the politics were different, we should join. One said it won't survive; the Italians will bring it down. Another said it will survive, and we should join now. The third said it will be reconstituted as a north European currency union; we should wait for that to happen then join. And the fourth – the economics fellow of Hertford College – told me over dinner after Chris Patten's lecture that she was a micro-economist and it wasn't her subject. So you take your pick.

In this context I note, on rereading it, that the Treasury's 2003 assessment of Ed Balls's 'five tests' for joining the euro is actually even-minded in its judgements, full of caveats and 'it depends'. Without much change it could have been presented as the case for sufficient convergence having been reached to join. It is the executive summary which comes down hard against joining, and you can guess how that was produced.

The difference between then and now, of course, is that now British membership of the euro isn't a choice, as we are heading for the exit. Then, in the 1990s and early noughties, it was a choice that was real, which couldn't be ducked or finessed. And it is now clearer than ever that the decision not to join has determined Britain's fundamental relationship with the EU, and France and Germany in particular, ever since. If we had joined the euro it is hard to see how it would be possible to be leaving the EU. In his chapter on David Cameron, Ivan Rogers argues that the moment we decided to stand apart from the euro was the moment Brexit seriously started because for the first time since we joined the EU in 1973, on a fundamental European project, we decided to keep out and thereby of necessity hand the leadership of the EU to Germany. After much reflection, I agree with this assessment.

There is remarkably little about the euro in Tony's memoirs. In fact there is only one paragraph in the entire book. Let me quote it in full:

> My problem with the euro was very simple. In principle, I was in favour and for me the politics were clear: better to join and be full players in Europe's economic decision-making. But I also knew that the politics were also very clear in another direction. It is, after all, as I used to say to my folk, an economic proposition. It is called economic and monetary union. Unless it was economically plain that it would be good for Britain, it was simply not politically sellable, i.e. the political problem was the economics. The trouble was the economic case was at best ambiguous; and certainly not beyond doubt. At the time of the 2001 election, I thought it conceivable the economics would shift decisively in favour and I was absolutely determined

> that if they did, I would chance it all on a referendum. My disagreement with Gordon was that he was expressing himself negatively on the euro. I was always saying, Even if we don't join and maybe especially if we don't, for reasons of diplomacy always sound positive. If the economics had changed, I would have gone for it. They didn't. And for me, that was that.

Now, the one quality Tony never lacked was fluency. This is perhaps the least fluent piece of prose he has ever published. I have re-read it a dozen times, and after his characteristically decisive 'that was that' I keep asking myself 'but what was what?' We have politics pointing in two diametrically opposing directions, politics as economics, economics as politics, and the more Tony urged Gordon to sound positive about the euro, the more opposed he was to it.

There is another striking point: Tony speaks as if the issue was resolved soon after the 2001 election, yet it was anything but. There were furious arguments between Tony and Gordon on the euro long after the 2001 election – in 2003 – and the issue was not finally resolved until Gordon's statement in effect ruling out British membership on 9 June 2003, two years after the election and three months after the invasion of Iraq.

I say the issue was 'finally resolved' in 2003, but in Tony's mind it was never finally resolved. Even after the June 2003 statement, he still thought it might be possible to reopen Gordon's negative Treasury assessment and hold a referendum in 2004. But as the months passed, this option silently disappeared without being explicitly abandoned.

In politics decisions not to act are as important as decisions to act, although the impact of them is obviously harder to judge. The decision not to join the euro, and the decision to invade Iraq, were the two determining international acts of the Blair government – an increasingly stark reality as the euro approaches its twentieth anniversary in 2019, the year that Britain might be leaving the European Union. Do the simple thought experiment: that we joined the euro but didn't invade Iraq, and you get a sense of how different things might have been.

And this isn't with hindsight. In my diaries, more pages recount No. 10 conversations and strategy sessions on joining the euro than any other single issue between 1997 and 2003, and that includes Iraq and public service reform. Actually, fox hunting is a close competitor, but we won't go there. At the time, Tony did not see joining the euro as a finely balanced judgement: he keenly, desperately, wanted Britain to join. There was nothing on which he spoke more passionately over a longer period – apart from New Labour itself – and it was a passion which many of us shared. It's why, until Iraq, Roy Jenkins saw Tony as the real deal, unlike Hugh Gaitskell, who at the critical moment made his dreadful, historically illiterate 1962 Labour conference speech about a thousand years of British history being in jeopardy.

So understanding why we didn't join the euro is vital to understanding not only the Blair government but the reason why Britain is isolating itself and disengaging from Europe, despite the fact that isolation and disengagement was not the policy of any of the eleven Prime Ministers since Harold Macmillan applied to join the common market, as we then called it, nearly sixty years ago.

In retrospect, there are two occasions when Tony could realistically have sought to take Britain into the euro: immediately after the 1997 election, and immediately after the 2001 election.

First, 1997. A vital secret of the Blair government is summed up by two pages of the Chequers visitors' book. The Chequers visitors' book, by the way, is a remarkable historical document for all governments going back to Lloyd George though it wasn't there when I last visited – I'm told because of FOI, which was Tony's least favourite legacy.

The two pages in question are the first two pages of Tony Blair's possession of Chequers, headed 'Saturday 3 May 1997.' On the first page are the signatures: 'Tony Blair' and 'Cherie Booth QC.' On the second page are the two signatures: 'Alastair Campbell' and 'Rupert Murdoch.'

Tony didn't dare move on the euro before the 1997 election because he was simply not prepared to have a full-frontal argument with the Tories and the Murdoch press. He thought it might imperil the election; but in truth, Tony never liked arguments to his right, only to his left, and the problem with the euro was that it united the entire right, plus Murdoch and Dacre. There was also the recurrence of another characteristic British attitude to the EU: the patronising belief that every time the French and Germans commit to something bold and very challenging, it probably won't happen and if we sit it out we can avoid the pain and get the credit for picking up the pieces. There was a widespread mandarin and political view before 1999 that the euro probably wouldn't happen, in the same way Eden was convinced the Treaty of Rome would never happen, and that if the Euro Six really did try something so ambitious it would soon collapse. The only problem is that the Treaty of Rome did happen; the euro also happened and it is surviving. The only thing that has collapsed is our entire foreign and trade policy because we bet the house on the French and the Germans being useless.

Anyway, on becoming leader Tony immediately committed to a referendum on any decision to join the euro and adopted increasingly negative – if hedged – language on joining. At this point, Gordon wasn't the obstacle. Ed Balls wasn't yet on the scene and Gordon was desperate for a credible framework to signal economic policy stability under Labour. This is why he had been 'first in and last out' on the European Exchange Rate Mechanism, of which John Smith had been a strong supporter, as he was of monetary union. Roger Liddle, in his excellent first-hand account of the internal politics of European policy under Tony, says that Gordon 'fiercely resisted' Tony making this pre-1997 referendum commitment on the euro. But Tony was fixated on the Ming vase and not slipping.

The pity of the famous 'Granita pact' – the tragedy even – isn't what was or wasn't agreed between Tony and Gordon about when one would abdicate in favour of the other, but that Tony and Gordon didn't concentrate instead on policy and agree a plan to join the euro immediately after winning the coming election. Instead, the 1997 manifesto had one paragraph on the euro: 'there are formidable obstacles in the way of Britain being in the first wave of membership if EMU takes place on 1 January 1999,' it started, as negatively as possible without categorically abandoning it. In case this wasn't explicit enough, a few days before the 1997 election *The Sun* ran an article by Tony under the headline: 'WHY I LOVE THE POUND'.

And that was that, not only for the election but for the crucial first months of the Blair government. I didn't work for Tony until 1998, but Jonathan Powell tells me that there were no serious internal discussions about the euro – and none whatsoever between Tony and Gordon – until the 'Red Lion Fiasco' in October 1997. Gordon's economic stability reform was instead to give the Bank of England operational responsibility for setting interest rates, an incremental change dressed up as a dramatic reform.

The Red Lion affair and the Chequers visitors' book sum up how decisions on European policy were made in the Blair decade. The Red Lion affair began with an over-egged *Financial Times* story that something might be happening on the euro. Tony, Gordon and Alastair immediately decided this had to be killed as a story. Gordon was deputed to give an interview to *The Times* saying that the government was a long way from making an assessment on whether to join. The words were carefully crafted and deliberately ambiguous, but once Gordon's media aide Charlie Whelan got briefing from the Red Lion pub, pint in hand, the ambiguity lasted about five seconds. According to *The Sun*, Whelan even suggested to its editor Stuart Higgins the headline: 'BROWN SAVES THE POUND'.

Tony immediately regretted what he had done, and from 1998 my diaries recall him constantly seeking to keep open an option to move on the euro. There was the so-called National Changeover Plan of 1999, except there was no plan actually to change anything over. Then there was discussion about preparing for a referendum in 2002, except there was no willingness to say anything in the 2001 manifesto or election that might actually admit this in public, still less prepare for it. We ended up instead with a repeat of the 1997 manifesto, promising a referendum on 'any proposal to join the euro', as if this unpleasant imposition might somehow be forced on us by a tyrannical Brussels.

The best description of Tony's stance on the euro is captured by this justification for his wider European policy in his memoirs: 'Though my general posture was pro-European, I took care not to go beyond what was reasonable for British opinion. This … allowed me to govern and to move things forward where I could.' Put simply, on Europe he was a follower not a leader.

Two further points about the 1997 to 2001 parliament. Stewart Wood's insightful chapter says this of Gordon and how he handled European policy:

> On the Friday before a Tuesday morning [meeting of the European Finance ministers'] Council, Gordon would call us in and ask what the main item of business was. Not atypically it would be final agreement on a directive in some niche part of the financial services industry, discussed for months if not years, and now agreed between officials after tortuous discussion. Over the weekend, financial journalists would be told that Gordon was fighting for the future of the City of London. On Tuesday, we would awake to stories about Brown going into the lions' den in Brussels. At the end of the Council, Gordon would march straight into the press conference and proclaim victory, for a deal that had been sorted out between officials weeks earlier.

This wasn't a Chancellor signing up to a national changeover plan.

Equally, other preoccupations had taken hold of Tony, particularly abroad. He fought two wars in the 1997 parliament – Sierra Leone and Kosovo – as well as overseeing two bombing campaigns against Saddam Hussein. Tony's major foreign policy speech of the parliament, indeed of his premiership, was his 1999 speech on the 'doctrine of international community', delivered in Chicago. The Chicago speech was drafted by Jonathan Powell – Prime Ministers came and went but the Powells kept the show on the road for two decades. In the shadow of Milošević and Kosovo, Chicago is the most convincing statement of Tony's liberal interventionism. It barely mentions the European Union. NATO gets far more references, and the United States looms far larger than France, Germany and the rest of Europe.

Tony is blunt about this in his memoirs. Europe was, he writes, 'brilliant at ringing statements of intent, which then evaporated into thin air when the consequences of seeing them through became apparent … In truth, without the US, forget it; nothing would happen. That was the full extent of Europe's impotence.'

And he says this despite what he regarded as one of his early achievements, the Saint-Malo Declaration, which raised the possibility of common defence efforts where NATO wasn't engaged. There was much hype but little happened. Indeed, it turns out from delving into the papers that it was only really a stocking filler: Tony had no intention to supplant NATO even for European ventures, but after 1997 he felt the need for a European project of some kind.

Just before the 2001 election, Tony, for about the twentieth time recorded in my diaries, told Roy Jenkins that he was going to go for the euro. Roy told me: 'Tony says this time he's really going to do it. He is going to call a referendum very soon after the election, whatever Murdoch does.' To up the ante, Roy encouraged his friend Robert Harris to write a column in the *Sunday Times* the weekend before polling day, likening Tony's record on Europe to Baldwin's on rearmament, citing Churchill's damning verdict: 'He was decided only to be undecided, resolved to be irresolute, adamant for drift, solid for fluidity, all-powerful to be impotent.' I remember Tony asking me why Robert was being so hard on him. I said I hadn't the faintest idea; maybe it was something to do with Peter Mandelson, who was another good friend of Robert's.

Why didn't Tony seek to join the euro – which by now was up and running – immediately after the 2001 election?

Memory plays strange tricks and can be very unreliable. In my first draft of this chapter, I wrote that whatever Tony intended to do on the euro after the 2001 election was rendered null and void by 9/11. But on reading my diary, I realise this is untrue. There were three months between the 2001 election and 9/11 – two if you allow for Tony's holidays – and there was intense internal debate on what to do about the euro in these two months. By 9/11, this debate had been resolved – in favour of doing nothing.

In an office note of 23 June 2001, Tony wrote: 'I see two possible openings for the referendum, autumn 2002 or summer 2003' – i.e. at least fifteen months away. At a Policy Unit awayday at Chequers at the end of July, I asked Tony what was his game plan for getting us into the Euro. According to my diary, Tony said, 'That's a good question. Let me go and gather my thoughts.' He promptly disappeared into the sun-drenched rose garden, scribbled notes, and came back to give us a pep talk at the start of the afternoon session.

> If we can we should do the euro in this parliament. I am absolutely clear how I see this. There are two sides to the British character: the cautious and the adventurous side. The cautious side has dominated us for the last forty years and done untold damage. John Major and David Owen epitomise it perfectly. It is the cautious side which wants us to wait another four to six years, to wait and see how it all goes, but I tell you if we do that – and I can already see all the forces of caution uniting, on our side also – we will repeat the mistakes of the past … We should do it in this term. There is no point being Prime Minister unless you take risks to do the right thing. If we don't go in, we will be a supplicant in five or six years' time.

I asked, if we aren't waiting four to six years, when are we going for it? 'That's a good question,' he replied. 'I'm going to think it through on holiday.' Which he did, and told us at another away-day, five days before 9/11, that it wouldn't be for at least another year. 'I simply can't open a second front with Gordon while I am doing the public services.'

So 9/11 didn't change Tony's policy on the euro. What it did, as Afghanistan gave way to Iraq, was to mortgage his capacity to do anything else as Prime Minister to George W. Bush.

This isn't the place to discuss Iraq. Suffice it to say that over 2002 and 2003 Tony's dealings with Chirac and Schröder on Iraq were first difficult, then impossible, and finally, virtually non-existent; and his attempt to impose a European policy on Gordon never got anywhere as Gordon took complete control of the assessment of Ed Balls's five tests and steered relentlessly towards rejection.

The key discussions between Tony and Gordon on the five tests took place in parallel with the key decisions on Iraq. On 23 April 2002, I record them spending an hour arguing about the euro, and Jeremy Heywood telling me: 'It is the first proper euro discussion they have had since 1997!' In early May, Philip Gould's polling presentation noted that the 'euro deficit [is] minus 12–15 per cent and there are no signs of breakthrough. Euro support we must win in key groups v difficult because of levels of disconnection, disengagement, asylum, and crime anger very high.' A month later, the journalist Peter Riddell told me that Gordon had told him that 'he wouldn't repeat Churchill's 1925 mistake of going onto gold, despite Keynes's strong advice that it would wreck the economy.'

Tony returned from his summer holiday at the end of August 2002 to tell us that he now favoured a referendum in 2004, with an eighteen-month campaign to follow a positive assessment of the five tests. This was a pipe dream. There was by now zero chance of Gordon and Ed Balls agreeing to a positive assessment. When Jeremy Heywood told Tony this in early October, Tony said: 'That's not happening.' But it's precisely what did happen.

A final point about the history books. A surreal aspect of all these No. 10 discussions about Europe is that they focused almost entirely on what didn't happen – the euro – as opposed to what did happen – enlargement and the decision to admit the first eight central and East European states in 2004 without the seven-year brake in immigration, which almost the entire rest of the EU decided to adopt. My diaries don't record a single conversation about the immigration issue and whether we should have imposed a brake. From memory, there was one short discussion, in a strategy meeting with Tony in late 2003 when someone mentioned Home Office advice that the number of Poles likely to come after January 2004 would be about 30,000 and it would all be OK; and we agreed we would go after Iain Duncan Smith as a quasi-racist if he played the anti-immigration card, as indeed we did go after Michael Howard in the 2005 election.

I should have known better and done better than this. As Roy Jenkins's biographer, and the son of a Cypriot immigrant who arrived in 1959, I was only too familiar with the politics of race and immigration in the 1960s, when the response of both parties to Enoch Powell's disgusting 1968 'rivers of blood' speech, and really acute concern, particularly in white working-class communities, about the scale of Commonwealth immigration was – to paraphrase Tony – to be tough on racism and tough on the causes of racism, in particular unrestricted immigration. In precisely three days in 1968, with cross-party support, the Commonwealth Immigrants Act was rushed through Parliament. Overnight this stopped virtually all immigration; in particular, it stopped the expected imminent arrival of 200,000 Kenyan Asians. I remember Roy Jenkins telling me that this was the most illiberal, but probably the most necessary, act to which he was a party in Harold Wilson's Cabinet.

The right policy in response to EU enlargement should have

been to agree upper limits on immigration as part of the treaties of accession, beyond which nation states could impose controls on the right to work. Having failed to get this right at their accession, it should have been done by Tony once migrant flows became far larger than initially envisaged. We had a lucky escape from dangerous populism in the 1960s because Enoch Powell turned out to be more professor than populist. Nigel Farage, by contrast, isn't at heart a professor of Greek but a professor of grievance.

Tony never developed a successful political project with fellow European social democrats. I say 'fellow European social democrats', but privately Tony didn't think he had much in common with most of them, particularly Jospin and Schröder, who happened to be the two most significant of the decade. The 'third way' was a political project mounted with Bill Clinton, not with Europe's left. It didn't help that the European left insisted on calling itself 'socialist'. Tony didn't think they 'got it' on the need to move beyond old-style welfare socialism towards the 'third way' of triangulating with the right and modernising public services – even though Tony's brilliance, as a social democrat, was the skill with which he persuaded the middle classes to pay more tax in return for better public services. Gordon has even asserted that the biggest tax rise in modern British history was the Blair government's National Insurance increase to pay for the NHS.

In the early months of Gerhard Schröder's Chancellorship, Roger Liddle and Peter Mandelson got Schröder's team to sign up to a version of the Third Way. But it was promptly disowned by Schröder himself when he was bitterly attacked by Oscar Lafontaine and the German left. The irony is that with his 2002

Harz labour market reforms, Schröder became as significant a moderniser of European social democracy as Tony himself; but by 2002 Schröder and Blair were daggers drawn over Iraq and didn't spend much time discussing labour market reform, the future of Europe or indeed anything else.

Tony was constantly amazed that Schröder managed to win elections and felt New Labour and the SPD were essentially different parties. He is disarmingly frank about this in his memoirs:

> The truth is – and I fear this was becoming increasingly the case in my relations with the European centre right – we had more in common with [Merkel] than with the German SDP … Their view of the European social model was very traditional. Angela would see the need for change. I liked her as a person also. She seemed at first rather shy, even aloof, but she had a twinkle that swiftly came through. I thought she was honest and instinctively a kindred spirit, and we got on well.

Tony was equally disparaging about Lionel Jospin, who he thought would be eaten alive by Nicolas Sarkozy, and he saw in Sarkozy a kindred unideological 'action man'.

The international political project which Tony forged in his decade wasn't with European social democrats but with George W. Bush. The worst thing that happened to Tony was the election of Bush because it ignited a strong neo-con strand within Tony himself. Jeremy Greenstock, who played an utterly central diplomatic role in the Iraq crisis, makes a highly revealing comment in his recent memoirs:

> The details of the frequent conversations between [Blair and Bush], and of the almost daily exchanges between their Foreign Ministers or close advisers ... amount to an extraordinary chain of bilateral consultation and debate, more continuous and substantive than at any other period of US–UK cooperation that I have lived through or read about, including the Churchill–Roosevelt relationship during the Second World War.

My diary contains an equally revealing discussion with Tony in December 2002 about the relative merits of Bush and Schröder. 'We stay completely with Bush,' he said. 'Just look at the Germans. Schröder knows he is in a dreadful hole now that he has lost the Americans. He is desperate for me to help him build bridges. We'd be loonies to make the same mistake.'

Tony was brilliant at getting alongside people when he needed to; and equally adept at ignoring them when he lost patience. He made a huge investment in getting alongside Bush, while paying cursory attention to the Europeans. 'It's not us that are destroying Europe, it's the French,' Tony remarked to me on the eve of Iraq.

This is Schröder's view of Tony in his memoirs: 'At the beginning of my tenure as Chancellor, I believed one could add a British component to the French–German relationship, making it a sort of triangle,' he writes. But the effort died in Iraq.

Chirac says pretty much the same in his memoirs:

> Having tried, on coming to office, to free himself from the control of Washington, Blair had not been long in bowing down to it. What saddened and angered me, to be frank,

> was that he did not make greater use of the former experience that his country had of the Middle East and of Iraq in particular. By immediately rallying to the American side, Blair unfortunately deprived himself of any real ability to influence the analysis made by the American government of a regional situation that it knew less well than Britain.

Chirac's words mirror the famous statement that de Gaulle gave in January 1963 to explain why he was vetoing British membership of the European Community: because Britain was essentially an Atlantic not a European power.

Looking back, there was more than one Ming vase. Tony successfully carried the precious vase of electoral success across the slippery floor. No one has done it better. But the European vase dropped and shattered, and the best that can be said is that Tony maintained a similar degree of constructive engagement that enabled John Major to negotiate a kind of British associate membership of the EU in the 1990s when both he and Tony decided, for essentially the same reasons, that they were going to stand aside from the euro and hand the leadership of Europe to Germany.

At the time, we thought this associate membership of the EU was stable. We even thought it might turn into something decisive if the euro collapsed. But instead it led remorselessly to Brexit, and now as a country we have to work out how to reinvent our international strategy from a position of failure and weakness similar to Macmillan when he took over from Eden after Suez.

For me, the most poignant commentary was the change in Roy Jenkins's attitude towards Tony in the months before Roy's death in January 2003. Roy's last speech in the House of Lords, in September 2002, was a biting criticism of the Iraq policy, which he thought utterly misguided. He told me privately that if it led to war, it was the equivalent of LBJ going into Vietnam. JFK was Roy's guiding star; in his view, JFK would never have got sucked into Vietnam and once LBJ made that mistake the best thing Harold Wilson ever did was to keep out while maintaining civil relations.

Roy's memorial service was on 30 March 2003, just after the invasion of Iraq. I remember it vividly because Tony had been due to speak – I had even drafted his eulogy – but at the last minute he had to pull out in order to fly to Washington to meet George Bush. It was in Westminster Abbey and I found myself sitting a few feet away from Margaret Thatcher. The most moving moment was when Sir Nicholas Henderson, a close friend of Roy's and a former British ambassador to France, read from Jean Monet's memoirs. The sentence I remember is: 'The roots of the Community are deep in the soil of Europe: they have survived some hard seasons and can survive more.'

We are in a hard season. Let's hope we can survive more.

CHAPTER 12

GORDON BROWN

STEWART WOOD

The EU should work as 'a United Europe of States, not a United States of Europe'.

GORDON BROWN IN *BRITAIN: LEADING NOT LEAVING*

On 1 April 2010, five days before Gordon Brown called the 2010 election, he invited Angela Merkel for a private lunch at Chequers. It was ostensibly to discuss the next steps in Europe's effort to recover from the crash, the state of Europe's banks and the Greek financial crisis. But it was actually a lunch to say goodbye. Everyone assumed we were about to lose power, and Gordon was about to leave No. 10. It was never spoken of, but it didn't need to be.

That day, Merkel had snubbed David Cameron, who would become Prime Minister six weeks later, by refusing to meet him during her visit to Britain. She was furious with Cameron for taking the Conservative Party out of the centre-right European People's Party grouping in the European Parliament, in favour of a new group that would collect a ragbag of right-wing populist parties – and some more sinister right-wing authoritarian parties on the fringes of mainstream politics.

At lunch she told Gordon how angry with Cameron she was. How he would undermine British influence in Europe by removing the governing party from the main party grouping. Gordon nodded and said: 'I'm afraid Angela that Cameron doesn't understand how Europe works.'

I was at the lunch as Gordon's special adviser covering European affairs. I'd worked with him in that role for a decade – first at the Treasury, then after 2007 in 10 Downing Street. When Gordon said those words, I remember asking ourselves if we passed that test, as we faced the prospect of the famous black door of No. 10 opening to let us out for the last time. Did we understand how Europe worked? Did we understand Britain's place in it?

I wasn't sure that we did. And looking back a decade later, I'm still not sure. Maybe it's because, as Madeleine Albright once said, 'to understand Europe you have to be a genius, or French'. But it's more than that. We shared many of the blind spots that plague Whitehall and the main parties' leaderships' approach to the European Union – on its institutions, its internal politics and the ties that bind its members beyond mere commerce.

Yet Gordon Brown had strong convictions about the way the European Union had to change to adjust to an unprecedentedly interdependent world, and the kind of EU (and arguments for the EU) that would maintain the essential but fragile ties that connected the British people to the EU project. He was also convinced that his leadership during and after the extraordinary economic crisis from 2008 onwards could help navigate both Europe and the UK through choppy waters and to a better relationship.

There is a political tragedy at the heart of Gordon Brown's time at the top of British politics. Having spent a decade working with Tony Blair to chart Labour's return from the political wilderness, Gordon spent ten years at the Treasury waiting, not always patiently, for a shot at the top job. But when his time came, his premiership lasted only three years, and took place during a time of momentous global economic crisis, with a domestic backdrop of political crisis around MPs expenses.

For a man who so craved control, he ran a country at a time when control was more elusive than ever. It was a period of all hands to the pump; there was little time or political breathing space to enact a vision for reshaping Britain's relationship with Europe. And compared to Margaret Thatcher or Tony Blair's decades in power, there may be an understandable view that there is not that much to see in Gordon's time as PM with regards to an evolving view of Europe.

However, that would miss much that was important and distinctive. Gordon is unusual in that during his time as Chancellor, he had a huge impact on our relationship with Europe – most notably through the 2003 decision not to join the euro – while the economic crash that engulfed us all, provided an opportunity for him to show economic and political leadership within the EU, and offered a taster of the kind of statecraft he thought was necessary to engineer a coordinated international response.

Gordon is a voracious and ferocious thinker, and a reader and a debater like no other politician I have ever met. At 4 a.m., we would receive the first quizzical emails of the day. At 2 a.m. the following day, into our inbox would drop the latest draft of a speech he would probably never give, that he miraculously produced himself during the course of an overpacked and stressful day, thinking through how to communicate an argument. Gordon wrote speeches to himself. Every day. To work out the argument, and to work out how to communicate it.

There was no respite with Gordon as your boss. It was exhausting. It took chunks out of us that are still missing. But, for all his faults, he was a Prime Minister who brought a brilliant intellect, immense energy and stamina, and a burning desire to understand change to Downing Street (both No. 11 and No. 10).

He brought that strategic mind to the question of Europe and Britain's place within it – what I want to do is assess his understanding of and approach towards the EU in three sections. First, I want to outline Gordon's worldview and the place European affairs had within it. Second, I will look at the characteristics of how he engaged with Europe – intellectual, political and personal (some successful, some less so). Third, I want to look at the strengths and limits of how Gordon saw the issue of Europe, in light of the unravelling of our country's European affair in the past few years.

• • •

Let me start with Gordon's worldview. He spent so much time thinking about how the world was changing. If you flew anywhere with Gordon, you kissed goodbye to small talk. Within minutes you would find yourself immersed in an interrogation about global trends or what you considered the great challenges of our time. He wanted to be a leader of consequence who faced up to the tectonic shifts in economic power and technology, and responded with a politics that shaped change in the direction of prosperity and social justice.

Gordon's view of the UK's relationship with the EU was seen through three lenses – economic, political and historical.

The starting point for most of his views was the same: the unprecedented transformation of economic and social life caused by globalisation. For Gordon, the fundamental political fact of our age is interdependence between nations, brought about by a revolution in trade, capital mobility and technology, with repercussions not just in economic life, but in environmental, security, political and cultural spheres.

Interdependence is not a choice, but an inescapable fact. As Tony Blair put it in his 2005 conference speech: 'I hear people say we have to stop and debate globalisation. You might as well debate whether autumn should follow summer. They're not debating it in China and India. They are seizing its possibilities, in a way that will transform their lives and ours.'

Globalisation means that cooperation between nations has become as inescapable as the condition of interdependence – partly because transnational problems require transnational solutions and partly for risk-pooling reasons. As Gordon puts it in his book *Britain: Leading Not Leaving*, 'building a shared future is our insurance policy against a risk-laden world'.

What is fascinating about Gordon's case for the European Union is that it is not based particularly on values, history or affection – nor is it a case for a particular kind of EU. At an economic level it is a case for a free trade zone, and at the political level it is a case for international institutions that can produce a coordinated, cross-national response to globalisation. In this sense, Europe is simply the first bit of the rest of the world that you come to when you leave the UK. Its unique quality is really its geographical position – its inescapability.

The case for the EU is that, flawed as it is, it is the only available structure for achieving Continental cooperation. In Brown's view, you don't spend your time investing massive political capital in wholesale reform of international institutions or their founding treaties: you make do with what you have, and you make them work to deliver the goods.

The second lens through which Gordon viewed the EU was that of domestic politics. To understand New Labour, Blair and Brown, you have to understand the eighteen years that came before Blair won the 1997 election. The emergence from the divisions of the 1980 Wembley Conference, the splintering of Labour into a new SDP, the disaster of the 1983 election, and the slow march back to credibility under Neil Kinnock. The loss of the 1992 election – in my view the most important and searing experience in the origins of New Labour – reinforced Blair and Brown's determination to do what it would take to restore Labour's credibility.

The yardsticks for Labour credibility were shaped by the difficult years of the 1980s, and the ways in which Britain changed under Thatcher. Put simply, New Labour saw the challenge as reconciling Labour to a market economy at home, and to a global economy internationally. And central to that reconciliation of Labour with market liberalism was making Labour's peace with a European Union that, by the mid-1990s, had become a single market project. For Brown, embracing the economic liberal case for the EU was not just fundamental to continued prosperity, but fundamental to reassuring Britain's voters that Labour was safe for Britain again.

Gordon also viewed Europe from a historical angle. Gordon was determined to avoid the pitfalls of previous national choices about engagement with Europe that had done so much damage to Britain. The most fascinating section of *Britain: Leading, Not Leaving* focuses on Britain's history with the European Economic Community before joining in 1972. Brown is critical of Labour and Conservative imperial delusions in the post-war period. And for him there were many: the reluctance to move on from a Romantic, but unrealistic, attachment to the Commonwealth, as well as the inability to see the economic necessity of engaging with Europe in the immediate aftermath of World War Two (Gordon accuses the Attlee government, for example, of a 'failure to distinguish between the temporary state of Europe – its debts, devastation and division – and its long-term prospects'). The Quixotic quest to make Britain into a third great power (whether through Bevin's Western Union idea, or the obsession with maintaining a role east of Suez at massive, unsustainable cost to Britain). And the wrong-headed view that there is a zero-sum relationship between the special relationship with the USA and closer relations with the EU – that Britain needed to choose between Brussels and Washington. That false choice, for Gordon, was one of the most damaging myths of all.

In contrast to these dead ends, Brown speaks effusively about Harold Macmillan's reassessment of Britain's place in the world after Suez – in particular of the Cabinet Paper 'The Position of the UK in World Affairs', commissioned in 1958. The paper includes a sentence that captures Gordon's starting point on foreign policy perfectly: 'In the nineteenth century, we had the power to impose our will. Now we have to work largely through alliances and coalitions.'

Of course, Gordon is no dewy-eyed Europhile. At one point, he quotes Churchill approvingly saying, 'We are with Europe, but not of it.' He also, somewhat amusingly, remarks, 'We will always be distinctive, situated between mainland Europe and North America.' (I looked up the distances involved: it is 3,700 miles to the USA and twenty-three miles to France.) But the dictates of facing up to interdependence, making his beloved Labour Party credible and electable again, and avoiding the catastrophic windmill-chasing of previous governments – all these considerations pointed him towards hard-headed practical engagement with Europe, combined with, rather than at the expense of, other international alliances.

So much for the strategic considerations shaping Gordon's view of Europe – what were the hallmarks of how he dealt with EU affairs day to day? Let's start with a familiar refrain in Gordon's thinking: the primacy of economics. Repeatedly during his time as Chancellor, Gordon converted huge national challenges into economic problems, and then provided an economic rationale to justify a course of action. He did it on renewing the NHS through the Wanless Report. He did it on climate change by setting up the Stern Report on the economic impact if the world took no action. He did it on immigration – ultimately less successfully – by justifying larger numbers of foreigners in Britain in terms of their economic impact. It is a version of what the political scientist Bill Riker calls 'heresthetics': the changing of a frame of debate to win a political argument with the public.

He did this for a combination of reasons: because he believed the way to the British public's heart was hard-headed economic pragmatism, but also, let's be honest, because as Chancellor it put him in the box-seat in political and policy terms.

Europe was no different for Gordon. He was convinced that the path to UK support for and engagement with Europe is built on economics. Again, Macmillan is the pioneer in Gordon's lookback at seventy years of post-war engagement with Europe. His speech on 31 July 1961 recommending Britain's application for membership of the EEC set the pattern, in Brown's view, for how to make a pro-European argument to Britain, focusing overwhelmingly as it does on the positive investment, trade and growth consequences of joining.

The economic benefit test also served to distinguish between European projects that should be supported and those that should be rejected. The famous 'five tests', assembled in the back of a taxi, were a clever way of marginalising the symbolic, political and diplomatic arguments for the euro, in favour of the economic arguments. And the disastrous flirtation with a constitutional treaty for the EU during the 2000s conspicuously failed this test in Gordon's view. He regarded it as a damaging, hubristic diversion, failing to learn the lesson from Maastricht, unable to appeal to the public on any economic added-value rationale. Gordon remained extremely detached from the constitutional treaty debacle – infuriatingly for Tony's No. 10 at the time – and was right to worry that it was a project that alienated people from its elites, with no public justification. And when Tony Blair decided that he would offer a referendum on the outcome of the treaty, Gordon thought it was a huge political mistake – and a deviation from the tried and trusted formula established by Macmillan back in 1961.

Alongside a relentless focus on the economic value-added sat Gordon's belief in what I call 'muscular intergovernmentalism'. His overwhelming focus in the EU was on the council, and even more narrowly on bilateralism and summitry between the Big Six (the UK, Germany, France, Italy, Spain and the President of the Commission). He had no time for the European Parliament, nor for the Commission beyond the President himself as an ersatz head of state. For Gordon, the EU working well meant the Big Six agreeing something, and driving it forward. The institutional interstices of the Parliament, the court or any other part of the EU landscape was for others to worry about.

In *Britain: Leading not Leaving*, Gordon refers to this vision of how the EU should work as 'a United Europe of States, not a United States of Europe'.

This 'muscular intergovernmentalism' was coupled with a heroic faith in shuttle diplomacy – his own shuttle diplomacy – between the heads of government of countries across Europe (and in the case of the crash, across the world). His style was to work out the answer to a problem and then present fellow leaders with the solution as a fait accompli, relying on the brute force of reason to get them to agree. It was a process he saw as the only way for internationalism to work: the accumulation of a coalition behind his grand plan, assembled by him talking personally to leaders.

It baffled some leaders, who started meetings with Gordon under the mistaken apprehension that there would be discussions and exchanges of views, only to find that Gordon had in best *Blue Peter*-style prepared the answer earlier, and wanted his interlocutor to agree it as a way forward. But it was a process that could produce results. Indeed, I think one of the reasons that Gordon had such faith with it is because early on in his days as Chancellor, he scored a spectacular success on the issue of resisting corporate tax harmonisation across Europe.

In 1999, the UK was facing the near-certainty of being totally isolated in opposition to the Commission proposal for a harmonised corporate tax rate across Europe, partly to reduce avoidance problems. Gordon responded by arguing that harmonised taxes would lead to large outflows from the EU that would hurt everyone, and proposed instead a new policy to combat tax avoidance based on exchange of tax information between jurisdictions inside and adjacent to the EU. With Gordon's muscular intergovernmental shuttle diplomacy in overdrive, a majority of fourteen to one against the UK on harmonisation became a unanimous decision in favour of the tax-transparency approach.

Gordon thought of this as his greatest EU-diplomatic triumph at the Treasury. He provides an extended discussion of it in *Leading not Leaving*, and cites it as a model for how to achieve the coordination needed to manage interdependence more generally. It raises an interesting issue about path-dependence in the way leaders see problems – the precedent set by early negotiating successes in shaping their view of subsequent challenges they face. Here is a more recent example: Theresa May's public remarks on a sector-by-sector 'cherry-picking' approach to Brexit negotiations clearly owe a lot to what she saw as her great triumph in EU negotiations when at the Home Office – over the cherry-picking of opt-ins on Justice and Home Affairs issues once the wholesale JHA opt-out came into effect in 2014. Her conception of how to negotiate Brexit was shaped by that success, just as Gordon's muscular intergovernmentalism was shaped by his success on corporate tax rates.

Gordon's shuttle diplomacy was extraordinarily vigorous – there was lots of shuttling – but it wasn't that diplomatic. He was a politician who fundamentally believed the world is propelled by interests, not by relationships. He was totally uninterested in chemistry. Relationships were, to use a Marxist term, epiphenomenal. If interests collided or could be aligned, you could do a deal. It is a worldview that made him, shall we say, unpersuaded of the value added by the Foreign Office, which with some notable exceptions he saw as a department more concerned with relationship management than with delivering government policy.

His indifference to relationship cultivation led to some interesting moments. On Gordon's third day as Prime Minister, we flew to Berlin for dinner with Merkel, to make a point that he would be taking the EU, and the most powerful leader within it, seriously. But despite the fact the whole point of the dinner was symbolic and relationship-cultivating, Gordon got impatient at the lack of substance on the agenda for the dinner as we were coming in to land in Berlin. He asked a senior Foreign Office doyen on the plane, irritably, 'What exactly is the point of this dinner?' The man from the FCO replied: 'It's what we call a getting to know you dinner, Prime Minister.' Gordon replied with an expression full of consternation and anger. He just didn't do getting to know you dinners. He didn't have the time.

On another occasion, Berlusconi arrived in London for a private lunch, during which the Italian PM spent an animated ten minutes talking about Roman Abramovich's new 75-foot yacht, aboard which he, Abramovich and Putin had just spent a lovely weekend. At the end of an effusive description of the vessel, Berlusconi paused and asked, 'Have you been on Abramovich's yacht yet, Gordon?' 'Er no, not yet,' Gordon replied. Yachts are something else Gordon doesn't do. Bunga bunga had met the Son of the Manse.

Economics, intergovernmentalism, interests not relationships: these were the characteristics of his approach to all matters European. As a matter of political tactics, Gordon saw most EU affairs through the lens of domestic politics. The vast majority of council business – first in the Economic and Financial Affairs Council (ECOFIN) when he was Chancellor, then European Council business when he was Prime Minister – didn't excite his interest. The point of a visit to the council was to show people back home that Britain was winning an argument, or a fight. And sometimes that could mean manufacturing one.

Let me describe for you a not untypical sequence in the run-up to an ECOFIN meeting when Gordon was Chancellor. On the Friday before a Tuesday morning council, Gordon would call us in and ask what the main item of business for ECOFIN was. Not atypically, it would be final agreement on a directive in some niche part of the financial services industry, discussed for months if not years, and now agreed between officials after tortuous discussion. Over the weekend, financial journalists would be told that Gordon was fighting for the future of the City of London. On Tuesday, we would awake to stories about Brown going into the lion's den in Brussels. At the end of ECOFIN, Gordon would march straight into the press conference and proclaim victory, for a deal that had been sorted out between officials weeks earlier.

Clever and perhaps just slightly cynical politics, you might think. Yes, but it also reflected a serious part of Gordon's view about sustaining a pro-European Britain: that the British electorate needed to feel that Britain was defending its corner, winning victories, fending off regulation that would undermine what was distinctive and successful about our economy. Maintaining Britain's commitment to the EU could only be done with economics, with wins, by what he called a 'pick and mix' approach to European engagement that said no to many integration projects (like Schengen or the euro) and sought specific carve-outs, as well as adopting an approach to negotiations that hugged the slightly Eurosceptic end of the pro-European consensus. Ultimately, of course, the positioning of both Labour and Tory governments at the sceptical end of pro-Europeanism came back to haunt the pro-European case in the referendum. When politicians of both parties who have been saying for years that they are fighting hard for Britain against the Brussels madness then turn around and say Brussels is a good thing, the public can be forgiven for being unconvinced.

This also raises a fascinating paradox about the kind of pro-European social democrat that Gordon was. Despite the fact that the great achievements of European social democracy, the most successful combination of prosperity, equality and social justice, were achieved in northern European countries, he had no particular cultural connection to or intellectual interest in the political history of post-war Europe. He felt much more affinity with the United States than with Continental Europe. And he felt more affinity with the US Democrats – its key figures, its history, its language and politics – than with any centre-left party in the EU. So when Blair and Brown looked to develop progressive policies for transitioning people from welfare into work in the 1990s, it wasn't Copenhagen or Stockholm that they visited, but Wisconsin.

Working as Gordon's political Sherpa to the Party of European Socialists grouping, I have to admit I often found this frustrating – not least because centre-left leaders revered him as a political heavyweight. On reflection, however, I see the logic of looking to the Atlantic rather than across the Channel with more sympathy. Gordon was aware of the different political-cultural context of Anglo-American democracy and Anglo-Saxon capitalism. His love of the US Democrats was emotional, but it was also an affinity with a party who, like Labour, were trying to achieve progressive change in a liberal market economy that made it difficult to tack left.

So overall, how successful was his approach to EU affairs? As Chancellor, very successful. The Treasury used qualified majority voting to serve the interest of UK business and in particular the UK financial sector incredibly effectively. The absence of the veto over most economic matters (apart from tax and welfare) was neutralised as a political problem, in the short term, by the sharp-edged, aggressive muscular intergovernmentalism that he pursued.

It was also a success on two issues in particular for which Gordon will always be remembered: the decision not to join the euro in 2003 and his response to the crash in 2008.

Gordon was not always opposed to the euro. Prior to 1997 he spoke in positive terms about the possibility of Britain joining. A story knocked around in Team Brown that in February 1997, before Blair became Prime Minister, Peter Mandelson called Gordon from a radio station in the USA, saying that he was about to go on the radio, and wanted for pre-election tactical reasons to rule out joining the euro for at least the first term of a Labour government. Gordon said no, that it should not be ruled out – that we should retain flexibility.

So what changed? Partly it was politics. Gordon's first act as Chancellor was to set up independence for the Bank of England over interest rate setting. Abandoning what was his greatest early achievement was not an attractive prospect, but while working on the euro decision in the Treasury (one of my first big jobs there having joined in 2001), I was struck by the way we approached it: the phenomenal secrecy that shrouded the work we did; the comprehensive, rigorous economics that formed the basis for the verdicts we gave; and the brilliance of Gordon's dovetailing of economic arguments with political positioning. It was Gordon at his best.

And one main reason for why Gordon and the Treasury agreed that joining the euro would be economically inadvisable was that they thought it wouldn't work well. Gordon genuinely thought it was not an optimal currency area. That countries would free-ride on fiscal policy, and that its design militated against counter-cyclical policy when it would be most needed. And that the UK economy, with its dependence on financial services, and its unique and dominant housing market, could not be governed properly by the same interest rate decisions that would be needed in Madrid, Berlin, Rome or Athens. Gordon believed the euro would not work for Britain economically. And if it hurt our economy, it would be a disaster for Britain's relationship with the EU.

You'd be hard pushed to find anyone – economist, politician or voter – who honestly thinks now that judgement call was wrong. And yet right at the end of the process, in March 2003, we suddenly got nervous that Tony Blair would intervene and overrule the economic assessment. Looking back, this nervousness was overstated. But it was a fraught time in the Blair–Brown relationship, with differences over Iraq, the euro and tuition fees policy combining to make things tricky between the two. One day, on the eve of the start of the Iraq War, Donald Rumsfeld gave a press conference in which he hinted that Tony Blair might decide not to intervene alongside the US in military action in Iraq. The next morning, Ed Balls, Gordon's chief adviser – and incidentally the most talented person I ever worked with in politics – came up to me in the corridor and said:

> Imagine this scenario: Tony decides not to go into Iraq with the Americans. He becomes the darling of Europe for siding with France and Germany and not the US. On the back of this popularity, Blair rips up the five tests and steamrollers us into the euro. What do you think?

I said I thought it was possible but unlikely. 'So do I,' Ed said. 'I think I do, anyway.'

If one great success was taking control of the euro assessment process, Gordon's other great moment came in the face of the economic crash in 2008. The events of 2 October to 9 October 2008 are etched in my mind. It was a period of turmoil. At one point, I was in a meeting where someone said it was not out of the question that soldiers might have to be brought onto the streets to stop a mass run on the banks. Gordon knew that the only response that would avert a continuing, cataclysmic slide in the markets was a coordinated global response – but it looked impossible to achieve that agreement. Each government seemed to have a different favoured response. The Bush administration opted for a TARP Bill, buying up toxic assets, while over that weekend the Irish government announced they would guarantee bank deposits (and the Germans hinted they might do the same).

Gordon's decision was to try and secure international backing for an approach that combined recapitalisation with guarantees for interbank lending. An impromptu summit in Paris called by President Sarkozy on 4 October didn't generate an agreement. On Tuesday, officials went into the Cabinet Room throughout the day, as Gordon prepared for PMQs, telling him RBS was in danger of imminent collapse. At the end of the day, Gordon authorised the announcement of his recapitalisation plan for seven the next morning – remarking that, if you do a bailout late in the afternoon it looks like panic, but if you do it first thing in the morning, it looks like strategy.

The next day the announcement was made, and a coordinated interest rate cut across the world's major central banks was announced five minutes before PMQs. The reaction was overwhelmingly positive, and Gordon made the decision to take the principles of the British plan and go global. That Sunday, he was invited to lead the discussion at an emergency heads of government meeting of eurocountries – five years after deciding not to join it. And over the next six months he showed energy, determination and stamina that I've never seen in anyone else in politics – inventing a new international organisation (the heads of government G20, with Brazil ceding the Chair to the UK early) to provide the venue for his muscular intergovernmentalism. Six months later at the G20 summit in London, a $1.1 trillion reflationary plan was announced.

Gordon didn't save the world, as Paul Krugman famously said. But he showed that in a time of unprecedented economic crisis, muscular intergovernmentalism could work – even for only a brief though crucial time. Yet this very success also sheds light on the limits of Gordon's approach to matters European and international, on which, in the spirit of honest reflection, I want to end on.

Oscar Wilde once said that the 'problem with socialism is that it will take up too many evenings'. Something similar can be said for muscular intergovernmentalism. On specific issues, such as corporate tax rules, or bailing out the world's banks during a time of crisis, the vigorous but painstaking work of building a coalition, one head of government at a time, may be necessary and may work. But it is simply infeasible to serve as a general model for how to do business across all issues. For one thing, the EU operates on a system of constant trades across a panoply of issues – based on a recognition that you concede on things you care less about to deliver results in those areas that matter. No UK government has ever been really comfortable reconciling itself to these trades – and Gordon wasn't either.

For another thing, the EU is much more than deals between the heads of government. Gordon had no time for Parliament, the politics within European party groupings, or intra-Commission politics. When he was asked by the FCO to intervene to back British officials for senior posts inside the European Commission, he rarely engaged.

The best example of where this rebounded against us was the appointment of Cathy Ashton to the post of High

Representative – essentially responsible for EU foreign policy – in 2009. Gordon very much wanted the UK to get a senior economic portfolio in the new Barroso Commission, yet he was hamstrung by two factors, one of which was Tony Blair's ambitions to become the first President of the European Council. In the wake of the Iraq War, and because Blair was from a big rather than a small EU member state, Gordon knew the chances of this happening were vanishingly small. Yet Blair continued to harbour hopes until very late in the day, and Gordon felt duty bound to quietly support or rather, not oppose, Blair's nascent bid, and therefore unable to lobby for another job.

After the Blair candidacy had finally died, Gordon found himself the prisoner of EU party politics. The centre-right European People's Party (EPP) and the centre-left Party of European Socialists (PES) had made a deal that the EPP would get to appoint the president of the council, while the PES would be queenmakers for the new High Rep post. The Blair saga meant that the UK was one of the only remaining countries yet to nominate a Commissioner candidate. And the number of female Commissioners nominated by other countries was shamefully low.

These considerations all conspired to limit Gordon's options. Gordon went through various forms of minor resistance – trying to get David Miliband to consider the appointment, for example. Eventually we were told by PES leaders that Britain could get the new High Rep post, but that the successful candidate should be a woman from the centre-left. By the time we flew to Brussels for the key PES meeting, this meant only one possibility: appointing Cathy Ashton, already a member of the Commission, an excellent colleague, trusted by Merkel and other leaders, and the favoured candidate of other heads of government whose support Britain would need for the PES meeting to be successful. Cathy, by the way, turned out to be an excellent High Rep, playing pivotal roles in important moments such as the Iran nuclear deal.

That was a case of Gordon being hamstrung by domestic politics and not reading PES politics in Brussels very well. In other ways, Gordon was straightforwardly unlucky. He fiercely rejected the idea of a zero-sum relationship between the UK's ties to the US and engagement with the EU. Yet by 2007, when he became Prime Minister, the Iraq war had driven a huge wedge between Europe (or at least Old Europe) and the USA. The constitutional treaty had been a damaging, self-indulgent distraction that ignored all of Gordon's rules for how to engage with sceptical citizens. And the combination of the crash and structural weaknesses of the euro meant that Europe could no longer provide the economic stability and prosperity that gave it legitimacy. The crash also ushered in a general retreat from international cooperation, with the exception of the 2009 G20 summit, making intergovernmental advances in trade or climate change near-impossible. The Copenhagen summit in 2009 was a particularly dismal illustration of the breakdown of the intergovernmental cooperation in which Gordon passionately believed.

These were not propitious times for cooperation between enlightened heads of government. Nor were they fertile times to make the case for Gordon's main mantra about the EU: that if

Britain wanted to engage with the rest of the world, investing in its membership of the EU was an essential first pit-stop. A man whose entire political strategy rested on economic justifications for international cooperation ran up against both the collapse in the ability of market economies to sustain prosperity and living standards, and the rise of a politics across the west prioritising issues beyond the economic. When voters started questioning whether globalisation was inevitable or acceptable, when anger about immigration irrespective of its economic contribution to UK GDP and productivity grew and grew, the New Labour worldview and arguments that Brown and Blair had articulated successfully for years suddenly seemed to belong to a previous age.

Now, ten years later, we are paying the price for a strategy of engagement with Europe that relied too much on a rather abstract argument about the benefits of trade and the EU single market for the UK economy as a whole. It was not a case that survived the crash and it isn't one that sat well with families seeing their incomes cut and living standards decline.

It's easy to look back and criticise the inadequacies of New Labour's approach to EU engagement, but the crash changed the playbook of politics in Britain across all issues, and perhaps the European issue most of all. By 2015, what had worked in 2005 looked like part of the problem.

But my one big regret about this narrative is that we never made a genuinely social democratic case for Europe. Our argument was not just economistic, pragmatic and pick-and-mix: it was almost always an economic liberal case. But the left's case for the EU, as I think Gordon knew, goes far beyond the scale of the market it provided. Of course the single market is an important part of binding the UK to the EU. But the EU should also be the best example of what happens when governments come together, and stand up together, against the power of global capital and multinational corporations. It should show how democracies can combine to impose limits on markets. At times it does this incredibly well – just ask Amazon and Apple, for example. But what a tragedy for pro-Europeans that in recent years, the EU's approach to crises in Greece, Portugal and elsewhere has seemed as concerned with imposing limits to democracy as with limits to markets.

Apart from on Britain's adoption of the Social Chapter back in 1997, I think Gordon believed that a social democratic case for Europe was too radical a message for a Labour Prime Minister to communicate to a public that was sceptical of the EU. He may have been right then. However, given the journey that the UK electorate has been on since the crash, I am not sure he is right now.

Gordon's approach to international affairs often came back to a fundamental question: how can countries combine to meet ever-more severe international challenges without sacrificing the sovereignty and control that their domestic electorates increasingly demand? Gordon's answer – muscular intergovernmentalism – worked for some high-profile, big-ticket issues. Yet ultimately, an EU of twenty-eight (soon to be twenty-seven) needs to develop a more effective model for transnational cooperation than the one Gordon was prepared to offer. Without the crash, I suspect Gordon's brand of intergovernmentalism may have had a chance to persuade Britain to keep faith with the EU for a little while longer. As it is, a Britain detached from the EU, frantically searching for multiple overlapping trade deals to compensate for the catastrophic effects of Brexit, would do well to find a Prime Minister with just 25 per cent of Gordon's energy, stamina, intellect and sincerity. We're going to need those qualities in our leaders very badly.

CHAPTER 13

DAVID CAMERON

IVAN ROGERS

The Conservative party must stop 'banging on about Europe'.

DAVID CAMERON IN HIS FIRST LEADER'S SPEECH,

BOURNEMOUTH 2006

If one looks at the Eurobarometer polling on whether a country's membership of the EU is a good or a bad thing, and compares the UK public's response to those of people in other major member states, one can see that the UK's line never rises as high as any of the other countries between 1998, the year after Tony Blair became Prime Minister, and polling day in the 2017 general election.

Deep public scepticism about the direction of the EU project and/or Britain's place in it is no short-term phenomenon. Had there been a referendum in the UK on the Lisbon Treaty, which emerged, misbegotten, from the tortuous process begun in the early part of the century to draft a new constitutional treaty, who can seriously doubt that the public would have voted 'no' and killed it – thus forcing, much earlier and in different circumstances, an existential debate over British membership?

David Cameron himself promised, when Leader of the Opposition, that there would be such a referendum, if the treaty had not already been ratified by all member states before he took office. By the time he became Prime Minister, it had been universally ratified, including in Britain.

Many members of his own party ignored the phrase 'if it had not already been ratified' and urged him to reopen the whole issue post-ratification. Cameron did not and could not. But what he did do was to legislate domestically, in the European Union Act of 2011, to place an effective lock on any additional UK commitment concerning further steps towards political integration. He clearly hoped to calm the Conservative Party's post-Lisbon Treaty frenzy and persuade it to 'stop banging on about Europe', as he put it, in his first party conference speech as Tory leader.

Cameron's own view, often expressed to members of his close team, was that very few of the great domestic issues with which he wanted the coalition government to grapple were much impacted by the EU, and that the public rarely viewed the EU question as among its central preoccupations.

In Cameron's view, the project to modernise his party and render it electable, after, unprecedentedly in Conservative Party history, three consecutive leaders had failed to make it to Downing Street, was to reconnect with what voters cared about and stop obsessing over issues most people regarded as tangential to their lives. Yet within eighteen months of Cameron's taking office, this strategy had effectively been destroyed by the Eurozone crisis.

One of the questions I was most frequently asked by EU colleagues, both as UK EU Sherpa, which I was from late 2011–2013, and as the UK's Permanent Representative until 2017, was why the Eurozone turmoil after the financial crisis appeared to destabilise British politics and policy on the EU to a greater extent than in their own countries. Many EU colleagues commented privately that Britain was surely in a rather comfortable 'have our cake and eat it' position, living outside the *machine infernale* that the Eurozone appeared to have become for them. We were insulated to a fair degree from shocks and better equipped with policy instruments to react to them, but we also benefited from membership of those parts of the EU which we had, over the previous twenty years, chosen to opt out of, and carve out a unique British status.

The reason for our destabilisation is actually quite simple. As the Eurozone crisis intensified, it became necessary to make urgent institutional changes to shore up monetary union and prevent disaster. But no such institutional changes could occur unless all member states agreed and ratified them. In other words, the UK was obliged to legislate, at speed, to permit changes that members of the Eurozone deemed essential to save the Eurozone, despite the fact that being outside the monetary union meant Britain would not be present at any discussions.

Simultaneously, of course, the worsening real-world impacts

of the crisis, notably in southern Europe, propelled greater numbers of people to seek work in healthier and more open labour markets, including the UK. And the persistent failure, as Cameron saw it, of the Eurozone to grip the crisis rapidly enough, led to very anaemic growth – or worse – which weighed on the UK economy, and exacerbated the challenges he and Chancellor George Osborne faced in tackling the UK's public finances.

Cameron turned up the volume, deploying typically vivid language about the need for a 'big bazooka' and for Eurozone politicians to allow the European Central Bank properly to 'stand behind' its currency. This in itself created tensions with key Eurozone players. Here once again were the Brits, standing apart from the Continent's existential crisis, insulating themselves from financial liabilities, avoiding all 'solidarity' save with Dublin, yet still feeling able to deliver lectures from the sidelines.

But in Westminster, the passage of legislation specifically and solely designed to cauterise Eurozone wounds and address Eurozone needs, inflamed Conservative opinion. The mood of many Tory backbenchers was that the Eurozone had become the proverbial burning building with no exits; it might be nearing collapse, needed our urgent assistance, and required treaty changes in its own interests. Many people were gunning for an immediate in/out referendum. But they did not talk much about free movement, borders or the European Court of Justice back then. It was all about escaping from the burning building.

By the time I arrived as Sherpa, succeeding Jon Cunliffe, now Deputy Governor of the Bank of England, the issue had come to a head at the European Council of December 2011.

That was very nearly the moment of terminal rupture between the UK and the EU, and its role as a harbinger of what lay ahead, and as a catalyst for decisions on both sides which led inexorably to Brexit has, in my view, been hugely underestimated.

The dynamics of the crisis were obvious. Cameron made clear he was no longer prepared to allow the twenty-six (as it then was) again to amend the treaties to enable the changes now required by the Eurozone members, unless, simultaneously, amendments were agreed to the treaties which alleviated the key anxieties he and Osborne had about the relationship between the then seventeen Eurozone members and the then ten non-members.

The concern was that vital national interests could be overridden by an organised and near-automatic qualified majority of Eurozone members. Jon Cunliffe was instructed to try and get a protocol to the treaties addressing UK concerns agreed as part of the December Council package.

In retrospect, the draft protocol was a remarkable document – it covered precisely nothing outside the world of the financial sector. There had been discussion of other issues, primarily the age-old Tory bugbear of EU social legislation, but none of these other issues made the cut. Cameron ultimately concluded he could only seek to address institutional questions connected to the management of the crisis.

There was a mixture of three areas in which the UK sought a return to unanimity from qualified majority voting to give Britain a veto lock, and three other issues which, though important, were essentially second-order Finance Minister Council concerns. The document consisted of several pages of dense prose on Treasury, Bank of England and financial sector issues. In other words, those issues Cameron sought to put on the table were not 'popular' ones: had the document been made public, one would have struggled in vain to explain to an average voter why they should care about any of it.

But these were first-order preoccupations. The aftermath of the financial crisis almost brought the Eurozone down, and forced it to speedily address issues of its construction and governance in ways that opened serious fault lines over conflicts between the financial stability-driven needs of the Eurozone, and the single market interests of non-members.

The UK constituted a very high percentage of EU wholesale market activity, with London easily the biggest financial centre in the European time zone – its growth and dominance in the past thirty years partly propelled by the huge legislative project of the single market, driven by the UK. How and if the UK could effectively defend its interests when it was not a member of what, to most others, had become the central economic project of the EU, which, in an existential crisis, they needed to quickly strengthen to prevent it from disintegrating, became equally existential for the UK.

But Cameron's attempt to lever open the negotiation got nowhere. Berlin and Paris essentially went round him. A couple of days before the December European Council, Angela Merkel and Nicolas Sarkozy, at a European People's Party (EPP) heads meeting in Marseilles, from which Cameron was absent because he had left the EPP, decided to circumvent a potential

British blockade of the amendment of the treaties by doing the deal at seventeen via a partly intergovernmental treaty process, which would not require UK ratification. The resulting Fiscal Compact is now known as the Fiscal Stability Treaty.

That decision was not notified to London. And it only really became clear during the night of the Council that a deal had been stitched up to bypass the UK, that the Council's lawyers' reservations had mysteriously evaporated, and that all other member states had been squared, so Cameron was on his own.

To others, notably Berlin and Paris, the UK's proposed protocol looked like we were opportunistically exploiting an existential crisis of the Eurozone merely to further long-standing British interests. The resentment was deep and the mood sour.

None of what was agreed that December proved of lasting importance. It was the manner of agreeing the inconsequential that triggered consequences.

In typical Cameron fashion, he turned this situation to short-term political advantage by representing it at home as him having vetoed others' desire for a change in the treaties in the absence of anything to address UK needs. He probably never had a warmer reception on a European issue from his own benches. He was lionised for having forced the Eurozone players to take another route.

But over Christmas, Cameron drew lessons.

First: the attempt to force permanent institutional changes which he thought the UK needed had failed. Others had circumvented him, rather than engaging.

Second: the Eurozone really did view their key project and interests as having primacy.

Third, and more soberly: his strategy had failed. He had gone, late, with a fully drafted document and many disparate demands; but the document proved much too complex for leaders to digest, and they were able to dismiss it as a ragbag that would require months of real work to refine. And it contained requests – notably turning clocks back from majority to unanimity voting, according the UK a de facto veto on things of critical importance to the Eurozone – which were never going to fly.

Fourth, although bigger institutional changes would, Cameron thought, ultimately require Eurozone members to reopen the treaties for larger-scale change, they were patently very reluctant to do so, and had developed a method to enable them to carry on muddling through without opening up a route whereby he could force UK issues onto the table. Cameron could not stop a repetition of the use of a Fiscal Compact-type device.

As the crisis intensified in 2012, and the question of Grexit (the possible departure of Greece from the Eurozone and the potentially contagious effects of permitting or forcing it to leave) dominated the spring and summer, the Eurozone moved more rapidly to start developing a so-called banking union – the only politically feasible institutional step it might be able to agree on, given the impossibility of reaching agreement on debt mutualisation or on a Eurozone transfer union.

Cameron was in favour of a banking union, provided it was a genuine one – and if the UK had no part in it. Those of us around him spent a large part of that year ensuring the use of single market articles of the treaty as a legal base for banking union legislation did not suck us into a project we viewed as intrinsic to monetary union. Again, this was not a theoretical concern. It carried huge taxpayer risks and generated inevitable political heat at Westminster.

Cameron and others around him had lost confidence in the views of those, most notably in the Foreign Office, who harked back to an earlier era and suggested he should seek a more central role in developments which he, rightly, saw as being bound up solely with monetary union and not relevant to our position – in the single market but permanently outside the Eurozone.

Monetary union radically changed the dynamics of the EU, and the impact of the financial crisis was to bring latent governance tensions to a head. There could be no case for the UK, outside monetary union and dealing alone with its own extraordinary banking crisis – bearing huge costs of UK bank bailouts and resolutions – to participate at further taxpayer expense in the resolution of the Eurozone's crisis.

This could be – and often was – represented across the Channel as in some way indicating a lack of UK solidarity at a time of crisis.

That criticism of the UK's transactional approach carries real force on some issues. But on these issues it misunderstands the nature, and obligations, of a monetary union.

For Cameron, it again crystallised the need to make even clearer that there were not two speeds of membership that involved everyone heading for the same destination, some via the express and others trundling by the slow train. There must be a clear recognition that viable, different, permanent destinations existed within the EU. And that not all were inexorably heading to a banking union, a fiscal union and a political union.

In reality, Cameron's position was the classic Eurosceptic one captured in the phrase 'common market good; political union bad'. Many of his Conservative opponents in the referendum campaign professed to believe precisely the same. But the idea of a single market-only centred membership, which many talked about in the decade before the referendum, has now largely vanished from political discourse.

For the UK, ever closer union was not the destination. And avoiding travelling there became important for Cameron, both politically and symbolically, but also substantively.

I do not know precisely when Cameron decided he would offer the public an in/out referendum. We were discussing it with him well into the summer of 2012, around G8, G20 and EU banking union summits, but the idea was gestating before that.

But this, then, was the context in the first quarter of 2012, when the survival of the Eurozone in its current form remained in doubt. Cameron thought that public consent for UK membership on current terms was wafer thin. He was clearly right.

Cameron personally deeply disliked the Lisbon Treaty settlement and its institutional implications. He foresaw major risks to the UK from the developing fault lines over the potentially diverging interests of the Eurozone from those of the Eurozone non-members.

His first attempt to address those issues head-on had failed. And he now knew that he would never get agreement to a de facto British veto on developments, by returning issues from qualified majority to unanimity voting. He was also aware that others had found a way to deliver the requisite short- to medium-term changes to the Eurozone without opening up the treaties to what he believed the UK needed.

Cameron increasingly came to think that he must not only address the Eurozone vs EU27 issues, but to deliver permanently different tiers or destinations of membership: hence the desire to take the UK out of the treaty language committing all to the vocation of ever closer union. So we already had, by early 2012, a high proportion of what Cameron ultimately tried to cement in the renegotiation of 2015–16.

For all that this held little interest for the public, and most of the media, in Cameron's view it had become the central issue of our membership. It led him to the proposal, made in his Bloomberg speech of January 2013, to attempt to renegotiate UK membership terms – to be followed by an in/out referendum. My contention is that his thinking about the key permanent changes he needed was set far earlier than other commentators have suggested, and was determined above all by his experiences in December 2011.

In the post-monetary union world, he was right to think that virtually all of the subsequent necessary further integration steps of the monetary union members would be driven by the imperatives of the currency union, not those of the single market.

This drove Cameron to think that the EU needed to allow, permanently, multiple different end-states for its members. He hoped others might be in the UK tier, but, frankly, he did not hold his breath on that, and he assumed the number of 'outs' would fall appreciably further, exacerbating the UK's problem if he did not fix things. The economic incentives of these others, as well as their treaty obligations, were vastly different from those of the UK. They might simply have no rational economic choice but to stay close to the Eurozone core. The view of some in the Cabinet that Britain might aspire to permanent leadership of some sizeable outer tier was, Cameron thought, self-deluding.

If the core then stood by the treaty imperative for all those without an opt-out to join the monetary union in the end, or leave the EU, the EU needed to make more concrete that the UK could, in perpetuity, stay, alone in its own version or category of membership.

This pitch was central to the Bloomberg speech in which Cameron went public with the commitment to an in/out referendum in the event of a Conservative election victory.

I will return to other key elements of the Bloomberg speech shortly, but first an excursus on the crucial subject of money and the UK contribution to the EU budget. A key reason for the delay in the Bloomberg speech was a major domestic blow-up over the issue which eventually figured so prominently on the side of Vote Leave's red referendum battle bus.

Cameron suffered a stinging defeat on the floor of the House of Commons in late October 2012, when his proposed stance for the impending EU budget negotiations – which was to advocate a real terms freeze, far below the proposal on the EU leaders' table – was rejected by a combination of the Labour opposition led by Ed Miliband, and fifty-three Tory rebels.

The political reality, which again reveals much about perceptions of public sentiment towards the EU, was that Labour saw the political opportunity of allying with Tory Eurosceptics to advocate a cash freeze or cut, knowing that it was unnegotiable, in order to have a populist stick with which to beat the government once any budget deal was done.

Most on the Labour side may have been surprised by the famous £350 million figure on the side of the Vote Leave bus, as the alleged savings from ceasing to contribute to the EU budget. But they cannot seriously have been shocked by the deployment of the argument.

But Cameron's defence, too, is instructive. He accused Labour of having given away half the rebate in the previous EU budget negotiations in 2005, which Tony Blair had chaired. And Cameron said, with some justice, that he was going for a tougher settlement than any achieved since Fontainebleau.

Facts are always hard to stick to, amid the emotions that the EU budget contribution and the rebate have generated in the UK debate on the EU over the last thirty years.

But I think two facts stand out.

First, the ceiling on spending Cameron agreed in 2013 was actually lower as a percentage of EU GDP, despite the EU containing twenty-eight members, many of which had been impoverished by over forty years behind the Iron Curtain, than it had been when John Major concluded the budget negotiations of 1992 for a solely Western and prosperous Community of twelve. Four years before that and four after Fontainebleau – in other words, nine years into Margaret Thatcher's premiership – the

Community had even resorted to a budget year of ten months to try to make the numbers add up. But British politics barely even felt the ripple. So one cannot really argue that the ferocity of the UK political debate is a function of the overall size of the EU budget.

Second, although the UK's net contribution rose dramatically just before and through the Cameron tenure, this was because the UK rebate was, in the 2005 deal, disapplied on structural funds spending in the newly acceded Eastern European member states. And the effects of that decision grew rapidly at the end of the 2007–13 budget framework period. After Cameron's election as PM.

For the public, the two most visible effects of the enlargement policy championed so vigorously by the British elite were something close to a tripling of the UK's net contribution to EU coffers, and the huge influx of Eastern European labour to the UK, facilitated by the Blair government's decision to open the UK labour market without the transitional periods permitted by the treaties.

For much of the public, both those effects were major negatives, and arguments about them played a heavy, perhaps decisive, part in the decision to leave the EU in June 2016. Vote Leave's campaign director, Dominic Cummings, said as much about the importance of the £350 million claim in getting over the line.

When the UK's pro-EU elites excoriate Cameron's decision on the referendum, or his strategy to win it, they must also, I think, reflect on how they underestimated the real-world consequences of enlargement for the bulk of what David Goodhart has termed the 'Somewhere Classes'. They also need to consider the extent to which their policy preferences, couched in terms that made it sound morally reprehensible to question them, fuelled the wider public disillusionment with the metropolitan elites, which partly explains the Brexit vote.

There was a great and serious argument to be made as to why it was in the UK's interest to bring in much poorer, ex-communist states, and be prepared to pay major sums of UK taxpayers' money to help try and speed up their integration into the Western world. But this argument was rarely, if ever, compellingly made at leader level. And by the time of the referendum, the fear of the consequences of further enlargement – even if the scare over the likelihood and consequences of Turkish membership was absurd – had become a serious factor in much of the public wanting out.

I would argue that Cameron ran a very smart budget negotiation, and one saw him, at European Council level, at his most engaged and effective. He was all over the detail. My point is simply that, though he delivered an impressive deal, it made scant impact on the politics of UK membership. The same, incidentally, applied to other issues – from Russian sanctions to the handling of the Ebola crisis – on which Cameron's leadership at European Council level was impressive.

By the time the Bloomberg speech was delivered in January 2013, the main contents had been well trailed with other EU leaders, and they knew the commitment to an in/out referendum was the central component. They were also aware that

Cameron planned to seek a 'new settlement' before putting the issue to the people; and that he wanted this to be legally binding, in order to prevent his opponents from claiming it was impermanent and readily reversible. So other EU leaders knew that Cameron was committing ultimately to delivering treaty changes in the UK's interests.

For all, the timescale on which he was promising to have the referendum – by the end of the first half of the parliament i.e. by late 2017 – was just not compatible with that demand, given that he could not possibly set the process in train until after he had won the general election in 2015. The Lisbon Treaty had made any substantial treaty change process much lengthier and more unappealing to the member states, and had given the European Parliament a much stronger institutional role.

It was evident that most EU leaders hoped the issue would simply never arise. Many – most, I think – counted on him not winning the election. Some thought, misreading both him and British politics, that, even if the Tories won, the commitment might be quietly buried.

There was consequently very little substantive engagement on the menu that Bloomberg outlined until after Cameron returned to office in May 2015. By then, the things he most wanted to pursue had been nailed down in the Conservative election manifesto. So the wise-after-the-event suggestions on how Cameron might have been bolder and got further with EU leaders by the time the process kicked off ignore the realities of the timetable.

Both Jon Cunliffe, by now the UK Permanent Representative

to the EU, and I warned in 2012 of the inevitably extremely compressed timetable to deliver any treaty change, notably with the timing of the French and German elections in 2017. There was just a brief window from summer 2015 until summer 2016.

Thereafter, we advised, the Euro elites would likely only resurface and at best resume thinking about major institutional changes by the end of 2017. By the time they did resurface, given the timetable Cameron had announced, we would be in the very last stages of a referendum campaign, with others consequently having no incentive – indeed no need – to move. They could time him out. Or force him to postpone the poll.

The quest for what Angela Merkel described as a package of 'surgical strike' treaty changes, which might be done under the so-called Simplified Revision Procedure, thus avoiding, as all wanted to, a full-blown Convention preceding an Intergovernmental Conference, kicked off in 2013. We spent our nights examining what could and could not be done under the Simplified Procedure, and what would trigger the use of the Ordinary Revision Procedure, the timetable for which would kill us.

Cameron had good grounds to hope at the time of Bloomberg that 'surgical' treaty changes would be a runner. But it soon became evident that Merkel's own shortlist for inclusion in any such package was running into huge trouble. By the end of 2013, indeed, it was clear that a German drive to deliver more binding constraints on Eurozone members' structural reform efforts was foundering amid French-led resistance.

What seemed merely difficult at the time of Bloomberg looked impossible by 2013 year-end. By the time I moved to

Brussels in November, I was focusing on ways short of immediate treaty change of delivering permanent, legally binding change that would be bulletproof, but which would still need translation into the treaties after the referendum.

I set all this out on process because, as we are again now rediscovering, legal form and process are critical in anything involving the EU, as indeed they are in all trade negotiations.

Political agreements, with highfalutin aspirational guff are one thing. Legally binding agreements, treaty changes and trade deal texts are another. That bind is central to Theresa May's own difficulties on money: 'nothing is agreed till everything is agreed' sounds fine until you discover that all that can be agreed is a 'framework' as specified in Article 50 – a purely political, not legal, trade agreement.

So much of the UK political commentary then and since simply ignores the reality of the type and ambit of the package that Cameron could ever have constructed at this speed, and got translated into a legally binding form. And for him, legal 'bindingness' and permanence was always key.

He thought that worthy aspirational blather, as he described it, on the need to intensify efforts on, and speed up completion of major trade deals or single market packages, or deregulation initiatives, would cut no ice with the public, let alone with his party.

This had consequences for the saleability to the European side of what he ultimately pitched for in the renegotiation. Some others hoped he would go for less bindingness, less emphasis on British exceptionalism, and more on pan-EU reform. They hoped he would use the renegotiation to expedite and promote policy initiatives many of them backed the UK in wanting.

But in my many conversations with Cameron on the balance between pan-EU policy reform efforts and nailing down UK exceptionalism legally, he always, in the end, came down heavily for the latter. And when it came to whittling down his list to what he thought was a manageable set of key requests – bearing in mind the experience of 2011 I have described – he always relegated the broader competitiveness requests.

Politically, I think this was because he thought the public could not care less, had heard it all before and were deeply cynical about politicians claiming 'the EU is moving the right way, thanks to British leadership'. For him, these would always be primarily just words heading to what he termed the 'European Conclusions graveyard in the sky'. They were worth little.

Substantively, he did not believe that any of the potential economic initiatives, however widely supported, would really move the dial on UK or EU productivity by the time of the referendum. Consistent with what he believed from the time he took office, he thought that in regards to nearly all the UK's major productivity challenges, EU-level action was not hugely relevant – either way. UK productivity did not lag far behind German or French levels because the EU was depressing it. Nor would it be transformed by things which could only be done if we left. Nor was EU membership holding back his government on employment creation.

And, frankly, as Cameron often told me, he did not really believe that most other leaders were with him on his conceptions of the policy and governance reform the EU needed. All of this tilted him towards delivering a more exceptional *sui generis* British status than broader EU reform. In retrospect, I think he thought he had put more ambition into the Bloomberg speech for pan-EU reform than he should have.

This is not to say he was not focused on where the EU could be much bolder on external and internal trade. He played a central political role with Merkel, in trying to get the Transatlantic Trade and Investment Partnership (TTIP) off the ground with President Obama. He did likewise on the Canada and Japan deals, and pushed a liberal trade agenda across the board. Similarly on internal trade liberalisation, via single market initiatives, Cameron consistently led the pack at European Council level. And, having started out frustrated by the whole way the European Council worked, he became ever better at delivering on what he cared about at it.

But he just did not believe that such deals, no matter how good, would be hugely transformative of UK economic performance – any more than he would accept that trade deals struck after Brexit will be. Whether this constitutes his version of the 'muscular intergovernmentalism' to which Stewart Wood has alluded, on which I also worked for many years, I am not sure. But I see greater similarities between, and continuities with, the Major, Blair and Brown approaches than discontinuities. All of them urged more openness, more flexibility, less rigidity, more Atlanticism, less focus on/constraint by European social legislation.

To EU27 eyes, Cameron would rank as much the most

Eurosceptic of these four British leaders, and indeed would be viewed as less enthusiastic than Margaret Thatcher about the need for a comprehensive single market legislative agenda – she, after all, sent Arthur Cockfield to Brussels precisely to devise the single market programme. Unlike John Major, Cameron had no desire to be at the heart of Europe. But he is in an identifiably highly British stream of thinking, which viewed the tackling of internal behind-the-border barriers to trade as the central economic objective of the EU, and which advocated muscular multilateralism and an aggressive regional trade pact agenda externally.

The radical British discontinuity, for others, is – of course – now. The champions of the single market for the past thirty years have now concluded, while rather comically continuing to urge the others to expand it faster, that they can no longer themselves abide living within that single market. The same reaction applies to British exhortations to proceed with enlargement: why on earth, argue others, should we listen to you, given that you could not, domestically, bear the consequences yourselves?

We are leaving the single market because of the role of the European Court of Justice (ECJ) in supranational, sovereignty-encroaching adjudication, and because we can no longer live with all the four freedoms which underpin the market project. We can accept the free circulation of goods, services and capital, but not that of people.

For others, ours is a regrettable choice, but a sovereign one for us alone to make. But one cannot enjoy the benefits of three other freedoms without the fourth. That issue, too, on which leaders will, as Cameron discovered, be as theological as their apparatchiks, will establish the parameters for the very difficult trade discussions that lie ahead.

I will return to that critical issue – free movement, migration and the Cameron agenda – shortly, as it became central to the entire renegotiation, despite being absent in 2011 and barely visible in Bloomberg. But I want to first consider another key component of Bloomberg: the Cameron view on democratic accountability.

Cameron's view was clearly and bluntly expressed in his Bloomberg speech:

> There is not, in my view, a single European demos. It is national parliaments which are, and which will remain, the true source of real democratic legitimacy and accountability in the EU... Those are the parliaments which instil respect, even fear, into national leaders. We need to recognise that in the way the EU does business.

This was a fairly conventional British position that could have been espoused by any Prime Minister since we joined the EEC in 1973.

As Permanent Representative, I kept expecting more fleshed out proposals to come from the Foreign Office, setting out in some depth what we had in mind by way of either treaty compliant or future treaties changing proposals for embedding national parliaments better in the EU legislative and consultation processes. Precious little ever came. There were some pragmatic ideas for how one would enable a proportion of national parliaments, acting together, to brandish a so-called yellow card to force the Commission to withdraw and rethink legislative proposals. That was about it, though.

Yet the rise in status and power of the European Parliament, and the change in the institutional balance – the Commission increasingly attentive to the EP, conscious of its capacity to bring the Commission down, and the relative toothlessness of the often divided Council – was, again, post-Lisbon, a much bigger problem for Cameron than it had been for his predecessors.

It was all very well thinking that the European Parliament lacked democratic legitimacy, and was a self-important talking shop obsessed with pursuing institutional aggrandisement, but it had, via successes in several Intergovernmental Conferences over a generation, succeeded in accruing real power.

At the practical, operational level, the way in which the Ordinary Legislative Procedure operated virtually across the board post-Lisbon, completely changed the game. Yet the British system still disproportionately focused its energies on the Council – because that's what ministers attended and cared about – and was only patchily effective at influencing the European Parliament's position.

At the political level, Cameron's crucial decision to take the Tories out of the European People's Party (EPP) group, and form a new group, the European Conservatives and Reformists (ECR), enthused his parliamentary party and helped win him the party leadership. He did it because, ultimately, he did not subscribe to the core political goals of the EPP for the EU. But it undoubtedly lessened the Conservatives' influence inside the belly of the beast, in which backroom deals and manoeuvres by the three 'mainstream' grand coalition parties largely dictated key appointments and institutional positions on major policy issues.

I have alluded to how Cameron was effectively blindsided on the Fiscal Stability Treaty by the Merkel–Sarkozy agreement at the Marseilles EPP leaders' meeting in December 2011. Even had he been in the EPP room, nothing prevented the key Eurozone strategy sessions taking place without him, of course. But the syndrome of marginalisation in the debates on the centre-right of EU politics, and the tendency not to recognise the extent to which the pitch had been rolled on key issues in party formation before the UK entered the room, was more general.

This problem went deeper than just the traditional British transactional approach to EU issues, which again was common to all British PMs during our time in the EU. And the mutual misreadings of interests and incentives which we saw in the renegotiation, and are seeing in even starker form now, stem from the absence of systematic informal political-level contacts which build understanding. Not many Tories now intuitively understand Christian Democrats in the way they did twenty years ago. The same is true in reverse.

I recall Angela Merkel saying in a bilateral in 2012 in Berlin: 'But your vision of the EU is so cold, David.' I think Cameron thought this was the pot calling the kettle black: from a leader who calculated, to the nth degree, the domestic political viability and consequences of every step she took at EU level – whether on the euro, Greece, energy policy or the migration crisis. But she also meant the importance of European political party family ties, which to her, as to others, are genuine bonds of solidarity that impact how far you are prepared to go for the other partner.

The emblematic case, which brought together the uncomfortable post-Lisbon weight of the Parliament and the importance of European political family affiliations was the appointment of Jean-Claude Juncker as President of the European Commission in 2014.

Cameron's primary beef was not with Juncker the man, much as he regarded him as the quintessential insider fixer type with which people, in his view, were increasingly unenamoured, but with the entire *Spitzenkandidat* process. This was the brainchild of European Parliament apparatchiks, which successfully confronted national leaders with a process that none of them really wanted, but which, collectively they could not effectively oppose, not least because, in the European party formations to which they belonged, their own party members legitimised it. Domestically, of course, it was not politically possible at home to say 'it is the whole process to which I object, not the man'. But to have succeeded in the EU, that was precisely what needed saying.

National leaders thus lost control of a nomination process which had hitherto been their sole prerogative. And for the first time in the EU's history, they were prepared to outvote by qualified majority, a leader who had opposed the process and was not prepared to agree the outcome of it.

Others calculated, in classic European fashion, that no leader would do what Cameron duly did: go down in flames in a vote rather than acquiesce and find a price. His calculation, on the contrary, was that to do anything else would send precisely the wrong signal for the renegotiation ahead.

It was again a complete mutual misreading of incentives and each other's political cultures which presaged many others that lay ahead. I warned my European colleagues in Brussels that summer – privately, but it was leaked – that we risked sleepwalking into a major crisis.

We duly did so slightly over a year later, after the UK general election.

For others, the outright Tory election victory in May 2015 came as a surprise, and the prospect of having to go through the renegotiation process was an unpleasant one. They all remembered December 2011. I spent much more of my time personally persuading people that we were for real, and wanted an outcome which reconciled their potential further integration with our securing a viable, permanent berth in an outer tier, than I did on any other issue. Many started with grave doubts about whether Cameron was in earnest: his personal diplomatic grand tour was designed to address precisely these doubts.

The Greek crisis, yet again, appeared critical. There was an unedifying attempt at a Eurozone Summit in July to renege on an agreement Cameron had, painfully, secured years previously to ensure that the EU budget – and hence UK taxpayer funds – could not be raided for bailouts.

The migration crisis was also intensifying both in the Balkans and the Mediterranean. Merkel's unilateral decision in August to open German borders to hundreds of thousands of

Syrian refugees sparked a huge and bitter internal EU debate about burden sharing. That the UK had an opt-out from the compulsory mechanism the Commission proposed for allocating refugees to member states added to the sense that the British were semi-detached, and insulating themselves from yet another Continental crisis.

For those whose crisis was one of uncontrolled mass migration of refugees from outside the EU, the British obsession with controlling free movement within it by EU citizens, felt like a sideshow. They objected even to the UK 'migration' nomenclature, which, for us, covered two issues that, for others, were completely different.

So the appetite to spend leader time on the UK question was limited, and the mood fraught.

On the two core primary law issues I identified earlier, which Cameron duly tabled as central demands, reactions proved mixed. The desire to carve the UK permanently out of the treaty vocation of the ever closer union of our peoples – there when we joined the EEC, and with the language refined by John Major in the early 1990s – caused considerable bemusement and some anger. It took a huge effort to get there in the final text for leaders. My personal view was that, while the political symbolism was clear, and the marker of a multi-tier EU as the clear destination was critical, the legal effect and potential real-world consequences were less significant.

On the relationship between the Eurozone 'ins' and the 'outs', Cameron's major personal diplomatic efforts to explain his preoccupations made the mood less toxic than in 2011. He achieved a fairly broad intellectual and political recognition that there were serious problems to fix here, and, in avoiding demands for a straight UK veto that he could never have got, secured the goodwill that delivered an agreement worth delivering.

The problem here – and generally, of course – was clear. The whole point of this central demand was to secure such guarantees as we could get, that our vital national interests could not be ridden roughshod over by a built-in qualified majority from the Eurozone voting en bloc to assert their own interests. But if this was the concern, then all on the other side of the table knew full well that leaving the EU would not address our concerns: it would merely leave us without a voice within the EU to prevent our interests being overridden.

This issue will shortly resurface with a bang, as we are hearing from Michel Barnier, when the twenty-seven make clear what they intend to offer in financial sector issues in the negotiations for a Free Trade Agreement which lie ahead. To state the obvious, they will offer far less on market access than we had when we were inside the single market – and with no real voice for the UK on the regulatory order to which those wishing to do business into the EU will be subject. No non-member of the EU or European Economic Area (EEA) gets anything close to what members get.

When dealing with the Cameron renegotiation demands they all knew that, as did he. This is why the alleged terrors of the threat to walk away from the table, which Cameron was constantly being exhorted to do by some on his own side, were, for the EU, so much less terrifying than advocates seemed to think.

Whether others fear you will walk away from any negotiation

depends not on frequency, volume and vehemence of threats to do so. It depends on whether the other side believes you can walk away to a better state of the world than the one you are leaving behind. And the people negotiating with Cameron held one truth as self-evident: however squeezed the British felt on their vital national interests by the strains between the Eurozone and the probably dwindling band of the non-Eurozone, it would obviously be impossible for the UK to secure the protections it was seeking – and which Cameron had been seeking for years – from outside the EU.

They assumed that the UK's desire for a major voice in the ordering of the legislative and regulatory framework of the wider European system would win out over all else in the end. We would not, to coin a phrase, put politics above prosperity. They are now calculating that if the UK's vision of post-Brexit Britain is one in which it concludes a plethora of free trade deals with other trading blocs and third countries, it is scarcely going to omit the biggest, closest trading bloc from its list. In other words, the threat to walk out and move to WTO-only terms with the EU must totally contradict the UK's own sober assessment of its best interests post-Brexit, and it can safely be assumed that the UK government sees huge economic value in not going there.

On the core question of the future relationship between Eurozone members and the 'outs', Cameron got virtually everything he set out to achieve. This would have been a highly significant step, had we remained in, and it is instructive that, as we leave, precisely the same issues are returning to the debate, raising questions about what we can secure from the outside. To which the answer will be: something very different. We shall be outside the single market, of which there is no partial, half-in, half-out membership.

Cameron achieved a set of principles (and a mechanism to enforce them) which established that those outside the Eurozone/banking union would not be discriminated against, and would not participate in bailouts; they would keep their own supervision and macro-prudential regulation, and would have specific provisions within the single rule book for financial institutions for the single market. This opened the way to necessary differentiation between those in and outside the banking union on bank regulation.

This reads like, and is, incredibly technocratic stuff. But it was critical for the governance of the country if we remained in the EU, and for the pursuit of the UK's best economic interests. No elite outside the UK was in any doubt about the significance and substance of this package, which further built on the fine foundations of British exceptionalism.

I have gone this far without confronting the critical issue of free movement of people and the control of immigration, because I thought it important to make clear that the decision to offer an in/out referendum long predates the point at which this issue became central. And to stress that it was the domestic and cross-Channel political tensions unleashed by the Eurozone crisis which put us on the tramlines to Brexit.

As I say, the issues of the relationship between the Eurozone and the non-Eurozone, and the question of how to carve the

UK out of an ever closer union, demonstrate that permanently different destinations were possible in a more flexible, less rigid union which recognised profound national differences, were there as cardinal negotiating objectives from the start.

So were aspirations for an enhanced role for national parliaments to rebalance power in the light of the rise of the European Parliament. So were the usual themes on the need to speed up progress on big external trade deals and on the faster development of the single market in areas seen – just those short four years ago – as important for the UK to lead the development of a genuine pan-EU market.

But you can search high and low vainly in the Bloomberg speech for any serious preoccupation about the operation of free movement. This was a dog that barely barked in my time as UK Sherpa. As late as 2013, post-Bloomberg, when we were discussing the broader menu of issues which might constitute ambitions for the renegotiation list, my recollection is that age-old preoccupations about European social and environmental regulation were always further up the candidate list; as were agriculture, fisheries, regional policy and a variety of other issues on the agendas of Open Europe and the Fresh Start Group.

Yet free movement ultimately became the thorniest issue of the renegotiation and a central issue for the referendum. And it is the decision to 'take back control' of our borders, coupled with the decision to exit the jurisdiction of the ECJ, which oblige us to exit the single market: the project with whose advocacy, alongside the enlargement to the East, all Continental elites associate the British above all.

I alluded earlier to the cost of enlargement to the UK Exchequer from the disapplication of the rebate in the Budget deal of 2005 to structural funds in the new central and Eastern European member states. The political effect of the decision of May 2004 to allow free movement of people into the UK from those states without the seven-year transitional period for which their accession treaties provided, of which all the other major Western member states took advantage, was even more critical.

Like Andrew Adonis, I recall remarkably little discussion of it inside No. 10 before May 2004. The official internal forecasts we saw of the potential numbers of arrivals were, as one looks back, laughably low, and became discredited within months. We should all have asked ourselves then whether they could possibly be correct. The one serious high-level discussion before the decision that I recall, because, as principal private secretary, I was there to take the minutes of their bilateral, was a meeting between the Governor of the Bank, Mervyn King, and the PM.

King pressed the case to open the labour market without transition on the grounds that it would help lower wage growth and inflation, address supply bottlenecks in a fast-growing pre-financial crisis economy, and help keep interest rates low. He made the same case publicly in subsequent speeches, when the numbers arriving proved vastly higher than had been forecast.

It is perhaps an underappreciated irony that two of today's most establishment Eurosceptics were, when in office, strong advocates of key European mechanisms, which, in very British fashion, they instrumentalised for entirely domestic ends. Nigel Lawson was determined to join the ERM, without ever intending to join EMU, to anchor UK policy and curb inflation. This happened, but the fall-out of exit in 1992 was a key component in the subsequent sceptic turn in Conservative politics. King welcomed free movement and exploiting first mover advantage – as no other major EU member state opened its labour market without the transitional periods – in order to tap a near inexhaustible supply of labour to address UK needs.

The economic benefits of the unprecedentedly large-scale free movement which took place between 2004 and 2007 were seen as axiomatic for employers, the economy as a whole and the public finances.

I am not saying that there was no attention at all pre-financial crisis to the distributional impacts and the potential impact on native workers' wages, and on access to public services. A different decision was taken by 2007 about the transition periods for Bulgarian and Romanian accession. But this was an immigration and free movement policy driven by the desire to fuel UK growth, and by the belief that we were stealing a march on EU competitors and further consolidating the advantages of the UK model over that of a sclerotic Germany, which we were characterising still in 2004 as the decade-long sick man of Europe.

Cameron told us he believed that the decision to open the labour market immediately, especially in circumstances where the other major players had not done so, was a big mistake.

Of course, he inherited office after the financial crisis, not before it.

I come back to the pre-crisis policy thinking and the fiscal position. In the Pre-Budget Report (PBR) of 2005, the Treasury revised up trend output by a quarter point, but only until 2007. In the PBR of 2006, they decided that this quarter-point upward revision to 2.75 per cent would persist in all years of the forecast. 0.6 was on the back of population growth: this is where the effects of the surge in free movement come in. Projected productivity growth was above two. This was a world of pretty generous increases in welfare and health spending financed out of healthy public finances, and justified by reference to that permanently raised trend growth rate.

At the macro level, migration seemed an unadulterated blessing for the UK economy, as well as for the UK employer class in 2004–2007. It no doubt was.

But, several years after the crisis, with middle-class and working-class living standards at best stagnating, the political issue which I think crystallised in the Brexit vote was not the macro effect – no doubt, inward migration was still a net plus for UK GDP and for the public finances at large.

However, the distributional impacts and the actual and perceived pressures on access to local public services and housing at a time of austerity became the political issue which electrified the Conservative Party and UKIP, but also the Labour heartlands, many of which were to vote heavily for Brexit.

When it came to the European debate, though, Cameron could not, to his peers, point to any serious economic dislocation here. UK unemployment was low and falling. UK growth, partly fuelled by migration, was healthy and well above the EU average. Where, his fellow leaders always asked him, was the evidence which suggested he faced a critical situation? It looked pretty rosy to most of them compared to their own situations.

Some leaders did lament to Cameron privately that many of their brightest and best were disappearing into the UK economy, frequently to work in jobs well below their qualification levels. But when he pressed them to join him publicly in seeking changes which might address their brain drains and his surge in migration, he got nowhere. There was no upside for an Eastern European political leader helping to stop individuals finding work in the West. For their citizens, this was, after all, the single greatest boon from the fall of the Wall, and of joining the EU.

I cannot, in this essay, give a detailed account of the renegotiation. But on free movement, where Cameron really started was with wanting to be able to apply quantitative restrictions to curb numbers of incomers, at least for a number of years. He basically wanted to be able to have the benefits of the post-accession transitional period, a decade late.

He hoped, when tackling leaders one to one on the issue, and explaining the unique conditions the UK faced, to persuade them that what he termed the theologians and legal Ayatollahs who recited the treaties before bedtime, and with whom he knew I consorted, needed to be overruled.

It is, incidentally, always tempting in the EU to think that leaders and their offices will prove less purist and theological, as well as more pragmatic and commercially driven, than bureaucrats in the ivory towers of Brussels. This is virtually never the case. The keepers of the true flame, and defenders of the integrity of the project, are so often the leaders, who always weigh to the nearest ounce the potentially fatal political risks of setting precedents – much more so than bureaucrat technicians, who may deliver the message, but are rarely the authors.

But it became clear, notably, but not solely from Angela Merkel in the autumn of 2014, that quotas or a so-called 'emergency brake' on numbers would not get agreement from the other twenty-seven.

It is arguable, I think, and I advised, that we might have been able to get some form of emergency brake – with a dual control key. But the dual control would have been a sine qua non, with the European Commission needing, in order to satisfy the twenty-seven, to play the central role in deciding whether objective criteria for the applying of the brake had been fulfilled.

For obvious reasons, that dual key was no use to Cameron, and would simply not have sold in his party or to the country. He therefore chose another route. He would impose restrictions on access to certain key welfare benefits by EU and EEA nationals for their first several years of residence in the UK.

That idea emerged in the autumn of 2014, after several months during which the immigration numbers and control debate had raged. UKIP had, after all, won the European elections in June and had captured nearly 30 per cent of the vote. In the autumn, Douglas Carswell and Mark Reckless, two serial Tory rebels who had defected to UKIP, both won key by-elections.

We were about six months out from a general election in which Conservative prospects looked far from promising. The whole toxic combination of stagnating living standards in middle Britain, continuing high levels of immigration and a metropolitan elite which appeared out of touch with real peoples' lives imperilled the success of an election strategy that was clearly going to be based on competent economic stewardship.

Cameron knew by then that any renegotiation demand, if he were ever to get a chance to table it, had to contain, beyond the elements I outlined earlier, a proposition which persuaded the public that he was able, while remaining in the EU, to address the question of the control of numbers entering the UK.

The outline of the proposal came from an Open Europe paper by Stephen Booth and Damian Chalmers and presumably got into the political entourage in No. 10 writing the key Cameron speech on migration via Mats Persson, the former Open Europe CEO who joined Downing Street after the election. No. 10 seemed confident that the public would view it as a substantial move. We were told that private polling suggested strong public backing.

This paper asserted confidently that the permanent restriction of benefits to EU nationals via a lengthy qualification period could be achieved by changes purely to secondary legislation, and was an idea that could fly politically with the twenty-seven.

I took issue with both propositions, pointing out that it entailed discrimination on grounds of nationality, which was obviously contrary to the treaties. It would therefore require treaty change, not secondary law revision, to implement a permanent deal. And it would not get it, not solely because there was no appetite for any treaty change at this point, but because this specific one was utterly unsaleable to Eastern European member states – and probably all.

This judgement would, unfortunately, prove to be correct.

And as Cameron engaged in his intensive personal diplomatic tour in the autumn of 2015, this became the single toughest nut to crack – though the ever closer EU carve-out and the work to try and hammer out legal protections for non-Eurozone players sometimes ran it close.

The deal that resulted, after months of haggling, and some exceptionally difficult leaders' sessions including with the UK's sole European political family ally, the Polish Law and Justice government, authorised a seven-year emergency brake which limited the access of EU workers to non-contributory in-work benefits.

This was right at the margins of what was legally doable without the certainty of a challenge to the ECJ. The entire package was as creative and bespoke as the EU gets. But on the most salient political point, it was hard to explain things in a sentence. And, as they say, when you are explaining, you're losing. If the cleaner – but illegal and unsaleable – proposal had allegedly cut through with the public, then this one did not. By the time of the February 2016 European Council where the final deal was tied up, the package was not selling.

Supposing that Cameron had then gone into reverse, told his EU colleagues it was not enough, and proposed they return to it later, (aiming obviously to get the question of numbers limits on free movement to the table) – which would, de facto, have meant by late 2017 – after French and German elections. What would have happened?

Clearly, the recriminations and accusations of bad faith would have been brutal, and there would have been blood on the walls, let alone the carpet. The package would, theatrically, have been declared kaput, and unrevivable. But that is normal. What, by now, though, would have been happening? One cannot know. Not least, of course, because the handling of the situation might have become more of an issue in the 2017 French and German elections than did Brexit which barely merited a line.

But I very much doubt it.

Emmanuel Macron has made public his view that the EU went much too far in its negotiations on the Cameron deal, and should not have offered what it did. I find it implausible that he, Merkel or others would, in late 2017, have been any more inclined to shift. As I wrote earlier, the self-imposed timetable of delivering a referendum by the end of what would have been the UK presidency at the end of 2017, would have meant they timed it out, or forced Cameron to commit to taking another year or two to nail the deal. I find it hard to see that having worked in UK politics.

Could we, though, by now, be starting to trigger a serious discussion of a truly multi-tier EU, with Macron's support? Perhaps. Again, though, I doubt it. As we are witnessing in the reactions to Macron's inner-core vanguardism, plenty of other leaders are only too keen not to go there either.

My instinct is that we would have had no resolution by end-2017. We would also have experienced major domestic fallout over the postponement, yet again, of a referendum promise. At best, we would be commencing a fraught debate about a broader treaty change, encompassing the ambitions of the UK and many others, with a hugely uncertain outcome and duration. The likelihood is that delay was a different route to the same destination.

Cameron's focus throughout his years in office was to defend and enhance British exceptionalism; he aimed to carve out a permanent niche within the market project, but outside the monetary, banking, fiscal and political union. He believed strongly that this was in the UK's best interests, and thought the post-financial crisis drive towards further EU integration would imperil the viability of the UK's position unless he secured permanent changes to entrench it. But he understood that life outside the single market project carried major risks and, by definition, meant we could no longer secure the protections much of his tenure was about entrenching.

He put those changes front and centre of the renegotiation for precisely that reason. He wanted to be able to advance the argument to the public, as well as his party, that he was delivering a version of membership, different from all other countries; one with which we should be comfortable and which was better than all alternatives outside the EU.

Cameron got most of the things that he wanted from the EU. And had we stayed in, those things would have been seriously worth having; indeed we seem to be arguing for many of the same things now. But we will find, outside the single market – where we simply have to be if we cannot accept free movement, and of which there is no such thing as partial membership, and with a huge financial centre which cannot live as a rule-taker – that these protections are simply not securable from outside.

By the time of the referendum, the politics had moved on, and even though the deal Cameron secured was valuable, aimed at the central economic and governance threat to the viability of UK membership, and in the long line of British exceptionalism, it did not prove strong enough to bear the huge weight that was placed on it. The decision was thus taken largely to remove it from the campaign argument and to focus on the 'project fear' argument we subsequently heard. And that, of course, opened up a new line of attack. And defeat.

CHAPTER 14

THERESA MAY

STEVE RICHARDS

'Brexit means Brexit.'

THERESA MAY, ALMOST DAILY FROM JULY 2016

From the beginning of her leadership, Theresa May chose to be rigid in relation to Brexit. She bound herself to 'hard' Brexit and was detailed when she had no need to be. Now, with little time to go before the Brexit deadline of March 2019 and her policy in tatters, she has become defiantly vague.

Like most of her colleagues in government and beyond, May had expected David Cameron to win the 2016 referendum. Showing a capacity for self-interested silence, she kept a low profile during the campaign on the assumption that she might be able to appeal to both sides in a later leadership contest. She had hit upon a third way: the Remainer who hardly campaigned for Remain. Even so, she had no idea her ambiguous role would pay off immediately. As well as assuming that Cameron would win the referendum, May also believed him when he said he planned to carry on as Prime Minister if he lost. In the early summer of 2016, she was unaware there would be a vacancy within weeks and that she would fill it.

As a result, she was not remotely ready for what greeted her later in the summer of 2016: the task of delivering Brexit as a new Prime Minister. The first time that she realised there would be a leadership contest, May was at her constituency home. It was the Friday morning after the referendum, and she was watching TV as Cameron prepared to deliver a live statement outside No. 10. Noting that Samantha Cameron was with her husband, May turned to the only other person in the room at the time, her then media adviser at the Home Office, Joey Jones, and declared: 'He's going to go.' She did not know until then that there would be a leadership contest in the immediate aftermath of a Brexit referendum. Even then she worked on the assumption, as many did in her party and beyond, that Boris Johnson would probably be the next Prime Minister. Only when Johnson withdrew from the contest did May realise she stood a very good chance. Suddenly she was Prime Minister when the only other candidate left standing, Andrea Leadsom, pulled out.

With dizzying speed, the UK had a new leader who had never been given cause to think deeply about Brexit. Her direct ministerial experience in terms of the European Union was acquired in the Home Office. May had not been Leader of the Opposition, a role which involves framing arguments and reflecting on the UK's relationship with Europe on a regular basis. She had no ministerial perspective from the Treasury or the Foreign Office. Her experience of the European Union as a minister had been in the more straightforward, though highly charged and important, area of security. On the whole, members of the EU agree that security concerns require coordination and sharing of information. The UK was respected for its willingness to share and coordinate. As Home Secretary, if May wanted to opt out of some EU agreements and opt in to others, she prevailed with ease. The Home Office tests many qualities in a politician, but it is not the best preparation for developing a rounded view of the European Union.

The 2016 leadership contest was the immediate context against which May had to make speedy Brexit calculations. The summer of 2016 was an exceptionally febrile period, and the Brexit referendum was not the only indicator of the unhinged political mood. In unprecedented fashion, both major political parties held leadership contests at the same time. Both campaigns were deranged. The Labour Party contest lasted three months and they re-elected the same leader. The Conservatives' equivalent lasted a few days and elected a new Prime Minister. Significantly, Theresa May did not know in advance that the Conservatives' battle was going to end almost before it had begun. She assumed she would face a second round of party members and would have until September to finalise her thoughts around Brexit before entering No. 10, if indeed she was going to win. As the contest got underway she was not to know there would be no second round. As far as she then started to think intensely about Brexit in the days before becoming Prime Minister, she posed a single question: how to win a Conservative leadership contest when a majority of members were strongly pro-Brexit?

Her early post-referendum discussions, which were confined to her then two special advisers, Nick Timothy and Fiona Hill, were largely focused on this narrow question: 'How can we convince the party that we are deadly serious about Brexit?' In reflecting on that question she began to frame answers that showed a willingness to aim for a Brexit in which the UK left the single market and the customs union.

As is often the case with Prime Ministers, the seeds of May's fragilities were sown in the period in which she rose triumphantly to the top. She had no time to think for very long about what Brexit meant. She had no time to learn how the European Union operates at the highest level. As Prime Ministers can do at the beginning of a reign, she made a series of rushed decisions. These decisions were the product of insecurity and at the same time overconfidence, contradictory forces that shape many early prime ministerial careers.

Early overconfidence in Prime Ministers arises from the fact that they have reached the pinnacle so many dream of reaching. At the summit they inhale a whiff of intoxicating power. The contrasting insecurity arises from the familiar pressures of party moodiness, the fickle media and managing divisions at the highest level. In May's case she was elected in the most bizarre of circumstances. She had triumphed and her speedy ascendancy was widely hailed in her party and the media. This sequence generated a degree of assertive overconfidence in relation to Brexit, at least as manifested in the approach of her senior advisers. But there had been no general election and no proper leadership election beyond her parliamentary party. She had also voted Remain. These were factors that fuelled a feeling of insecurity.

In reality, May had no immediate cause to feel insecure in relation to the Brexiteers in her parliamentary party and the media. There was not going to be another leadership contest in the months that followed. She was walking on water according to the opinion polls. But she felt a need to reassure them much more than she did the Remainers in the Conservative Party.

May's contrasting overconfidence triggered a purge in No. 10 and the Treasury of more or less anyone associated with David Cameron, George Osborne and the EU. The purge had many consequences but one of the more overlooked was a sudden loss of a collective memory in relation to the European Union. The mistakes Cameron made in his renegotiation with the EU and the lessons learnt from that negotiation would have been invaluable to a novice Prime Minister exposed suddenly to the task of Brexit. Merely to have one or two officials or ministers involved in the torrid twists and turns of the late Cameron era in the room with May and her advisers when they were having early conversations about Brexit might have made May's approach more agile. Instead, those who had learnt lessons from Cameron's renegotiation were largely in exile. She was confident – and foolish – enough to sack them.

The overconfidence also took an early ideological form. Her senior adviser, Nick Timothy, is credited or blamed for May's occasional displays of ideological zeal. As an adviser Timothy was a distinctive and interesting blend, combining a hint of Enoch Powell's Midlands' nationalism and Ed Miliband's faith in the state. He was a genuine radical and innovative thinker who was also a committed Brexiteer. There is speculation as to whether May was a mere vessel for Timothy's ideas or whether she also shared his distinct values. In terms of her actions, she appears to have shared them erratically.

At an early stage of May's tenure the newly appointed Chancellor, Philip Hammond, stressed to her the importance of the financial sector to the UK economy and argued that a key Brexit priority must be to protect the City of London from sweeping changes. May did not altogether concur. She told Hammond that the UK had been far too dependent on the financial sector for too long, and that she saw Brexit partly as an opportunity to recalibrate the British economy. This was ideological overconfidence of a rare order. The Treasury was aghast.

So from the beginning May's course was set. She had voted Remain and felt she had to prove she would implement Brexit. This needless defensiveness was combined with an overconfident ideological zeal slightly at odds with her personality.

Her ministerial team was equally ill prepared. Her Brexit Secretary, David Davis, had never been a Cabinet minister. He had been a highly effective Europe minister in the 1990s but the EU had changed beyond recognition since then. Boris Johnson had also never been a Cabinet minister before moving to one of the top jobs in government at the Foreign Office. Liam Fox had been forced to resign as Defence Secretary under David Cameron and now became the key figure seeking future trade deals. To some extent, all of them mistakenly regarded the early stages of the negotiation as a game of poker. The EU took a more direct approach. It published its objectives soon after May triggered Article 50 in March 2017 and told its key negotiators to meet them. The rest of the EU viewed Brexit as a process to be managed during which its rules and institutions would be protected from the trauma of one country leaving. In contrast British ministers declared publicly, and more pugnaciously in private, that German car manufacturers and other EU exporters would demand a different type of deal with the UK than the one the EU sought. There was an early machismo and much talk of cards being played once the talks began, as if the ace of spades was up their sleeve.

With Cameron's allies no longer around to point to the dangers, May and Davis repeated an error made by Cameron in his attempted renegotiation. Cameron assumed he could make headway by conducting one-to-one negotiations with some of the key EU leaders, and that he could challenge the Commission's overall negotiating stance by playing one leader off against the other. May and Davis entertained exactly the same false hopes. Journalists were briefed that UK ministers were highly confident of making alliances with key EU countries which would break away from the Commission's negotiating brief. May and Davis displayed a misunderstanding of the way the European Union worked and it was precisely the same mistake that Cameron had made.

These were the assumptions and the context as May made her early moves. When Harold Wilson twisted and turned in relation to Europe he managed to 'keep all options open', to revive one of his favourite phrases. John Major seemed weak at times but he traded a reputation for 'weak leadership' in order to retain some flexibility in relation to Europe. At his peak Tony Blair managed to simultaneously oppose and support the single currency, while also appearing decisive. For a time David Cameron kept the show on the road by offering a referendum. May managed to trap herself very early on. Her first soundbite on the issue was mouthed in the summer of 2016, even before she had uttered the banality that 'Brexit means Brexit'. May declared that the ending of free movement was 'a red line' in the forthcoming negotiation. She did not choose to follow through the implications of that early statement but they were clear and unavoidable. Her red line signalled that the UK would no longer be in the single market and the customs union.

But initially May struggled to frame an argument around her chosen course. Instead she insisted she did not want 'a running commentary', a comically unrealistic expectation. Again she had been formed by her experience at the Home Office. In her previous job she was accustomed to making policy without great public scrutiny. She often turned down interviews on the *Today* programme and *The Andrew Marr Show* as she navigated her course. She assumed wrongly that she could get away with a similar evasiveness in relation to the most significant change in UK policy since 1945. Her public reticence was also the consequence of her most fundamental contortion: she was leading the UK towards a destination that she had opposed a few months earlier. May decided that her ultimate duty was to implement the outcome of the referendum. But she also knew that the 'wishes of the British people' might have perilous consequences, or she would not have voted Remain. She struggled to make public sense of the contortion. Asked several times whether she would vote for Brexit if there was another referendum, she could not answer directly or artfully. She merely said there would be no second referendum, the answer to a different question. She was not a 'teacher' Prime Minister with language and performance skills.

May chose to be trapped in stages. Having declared that the end of free movement was a red line, the next key step towards her incarceration was a special speech she delivered on Brexit at the start of the Conservative Party conference in October 2016. It was during this address that she pledged to trigger Article 50 by the end of the following March. She made the pledge not because she had a clear idea of the route ahead once Article 50 had been triggered. She was not clear about the route and had not even begun to resolve the internal differences in her Cabinet over the route ahead. Like so many previous Prime Ministers in relation to Europe, May acted for reasons of party management. Unlike previous Prime Ministers, though, she was triggering a timetable from which there was no escape.

Throughout the summer Conservative MPs had been popping up asking why she had not already triggered Article 50. In response to their demands May thought she had hit upon a balanced approach, another Blair-like third way. She rationalised that she did not trigger Article 50 immediately after becoming Prime Minister, as some of her MPs had wanted, but she was also assuring impatient backbenchers and newspapers that they would not have to wait beyond 31 March of the following year. Excited Eurosceptic newspapers hailed her third way as a Thatcher-like act of assertion. The opposite was closer to the truth. May could have waited longer and a delay would have been a display of courageous strength. Well ahead in the opinion polls, she was in a strong enough position to resolve at least some of the internal differences within her Cabinet before starting the clock. Instead the clock was ticking without any resolution as to the means of achieving her sugary objectives of leaving the EU, while also retaining the benefits of the EU and agreeing trade deals elsewhere. During the same party conference May confirmed that the UK would leave the jurisdiction of the European Court, a policy that had previously been implicit. But even at this point, the autumn of 2017, she did not state explicitly that the UK would leave the single market and the customs union.

She did so, more or less, in her Lancaster House speech of January 2017. But even then there was an ambiguity running through her careful words, a speech that was still being written and rewritten the day before it was delivered. May spoke about the possibility of 'associate membership' of the customs union. There are associate members of tennis clubs who never seem to be able to book a court. The imprecise term papered over the cracks. May was smart enough to realise the calamitous consequences of a complete break with the customs union, yet she needed to declare and genuinely wanted to assert that the UK would negotiate its own deals. Liam Fox and others had convinced her that countries were queuing up to sign new deals.

Around the time she delivered her Lancaster House speech, David Davis advised May to call an early election. Davis said there were two reasons why an early vote made sense. Most obviously, the bigger majority that he assumed would follow the election would make the legislative path much more straightforward. Of equal importance, as far as he was concerned, was that an election in 2017 meant there would be no need for another one in the immediate aftermath of Brexit. Instead the government could breathe until 2022.

May listened to Davis and gave no indication of what she was thinking. As far as she was concerned the unexpected trauma of the Budget in March 2017 was a key step towards her fateful decision. The government faced defeat on a Budget proposal to increase National Insurance for small businesses, a policy that was in defiance of the 2015 Conservative Party manifesto. Within days it was forced to announce a U-turn. May and her Chancellor Philip Hammond were constrained by a manifesto which they had played no part in composing. Hammond was another who urged May to call an election and secure her own mandate. May had sought liberation from the Cameron era from the beginning of her reign. An early election on her own manifesto would be a big leap towards the new political freedom that she sought. Assuming the opinion polls were correct, she expected to win a substantial majority that would seal her dominance of British politics for years to come.

The early election of 8 June 2017 had a Shakespearean quality.

May is not to be compared with King Lear or Macbeth in terms of her shy and publicly awkward personality but there are parallels with Shakespeare's tragic heroes. Shakespeare had a theory, widely held at the time he was writing, that if leaders break with the natural order of things they unleash forces that turn on them. Macbeth killed Duncan to seize the crown and triggered a sequence of events that ultimately destroyed him. Lear broke up his estate and became homeless. May called an early election in order to win big and almost lost. May had declared several times that she would not call an early election, but in the end she succumbed and called one. Expecting a sizeable majority to reinforce her dominance, instead she unleashed forces that turned on her. The early election transformed the politics of Brexit under May. At the start of the campaign, May had stated explicitly that she was seeking a mandate for her version of Brexit. She failed to win such a mandate. The House of Lords in particular no longer felt bound to support all aspects of her Brexit plans, but critics in the Commons could also claim legitimately that May did not have the majority that she had sought.

Voters in the United Kingdom tend to elect Prime Ministers who are partly actors, and although the public and much of the media claim to dislike the artifice of politics, they need the artistry. Margaret Thatcher was an actress. She was nowhere near as self-confident as her public stridency suggested. Tony Blair could have acted the parts of Macbeth and Hamlet simultaneously. David Cameron was an imitator of Tony Blair, almost consciously an impressionist like Rory Bremner. These Prime Ministers were all fascinated by their place on the political stage, and on how they appeared at any given time. May was not interested in politics as a performance. Her shyness and awkwardness are in some respects endearing. She is not mesmerised by the glamour and glitter of politics. In spite of May's reticence, some of her expensively hired strategists made the election about her. But she was wholly unsuited to such a personal focus. When she appeared on *The One Show* on BBC 1, for the softest interview ever given in the Western world, the toughest question she had to answer was 'who puts out the rubbish at night?' May gave a fleeting look of horror, as if she'd just been asked to reveal her whole hand in the Brexit negotiations. She was uneasy in the presidential-type contest that the June election became and, in a sensational twist, she lost her parliamentary majority.

Voters can be fickle, but their change of mood towards her was quicker and therefore more traumatic than any Prime Minister had endured in recent decades. Before the election, when May decreed whatever she chose to decree on Brexit, she was unchallenged by her Cabinet. She was the only person in the Cabinet who wanted to include student numbers in the immigration figures. Cabinet ministers noted her determination to include figures that distorted perceptions of immigration, but they did not dare to defy her. Amber Rudd, then a new liberal Home Secretary in 2016, read an illiberal party conference speech that she did not fully believe in. Rudd had just been appointed. She uttered words that May wanted her to speak. In contrast, at the post-election party conference in 2017, Rudd delivered a distinctly more liberal speech, one she was more at ease with. Rudd remained wary of challenging May, but the difference in the two speeches was a demonstration of how power had been removed from the Prime Minister by the trauma of the election.

After the election May faced Brexit with no overall parliamentary majority. Her fragility was unique. Normally when Prime Ministers lose their overall majorities, they cease to be Prime Minister. Ted Heath is another Prime Minister who called a 'Shakespearean' early election only to find forces turning on him. In February 1974 he lost his overall majority, tried to stay on, but was gone by the Monday. Although Harold Wilson then took over as a minority Prime Minister, he was viewed as a victor. In her case, May was deemed to have lost. And it is in this context that she has to navigate Brexit.

In one respect her new vulnerability changed nothing. One of the ironies of Brexit is that, although the election was a turning point, in some ways it was not. If May had won a landslide she would still need to overcome huge problems to deliver objectives described by one ministerial adviser as 'having your cake and eating it', the essence of May's position. She still would have found the negotiations almost impossible and still would have had to make the Florence Speech, her address at the end of September 2017 on the eve of the party conference season. Her Florence Speech was not aimed so much at the Conservative Party. May's latest words were aimed at securing a breakthrough in the European Union, as she started to realise that the early flourishes of UK machismo were wholly unrealisable. Tonally, the speech was conciliatory and internationalist. May agreed that the UK would pay a Brexit bill, the sum conveniently being left unspecified. In interviews surrounding the speech she made clear what was implicit in it. She ached for a deal. The UK machismo around a 'no deal' had gone.

The wider political context explains quite a lot of what has happened during May's leadership. She inherited a thorny crown. She was a Remainer committed to delivering Brexit, with hardliners in her party and the media neurotically alert to any signs of betrayal. May inherited a tiny majority and then lost it in an election. But the character of a leader also matters hugely at such febrile times. May is often described as 'weak'. The term is close to useless in casting light on a leader, but as far as it means anything it points us in the wrong direction. May is the most stubborn Prime Minister to occupy No. 10 for many decades, arguably even more stubborn than Margaret Thatcher. Often Thatcher was more expedient than she seemed. May is a stubborn leader in a weak position, a potentially explosive combination.

Indeed May mistakes being stubborn for integrity. If she is committed publicly to an absurd immigration target, she must stick to it. If she has said that the UK will leave the single market and the customs union, the UK must depart at the assigned date. She is not a leader of guile, who might set a long-term goal and then act with slipperiness, the end justifying the means. May's aims in relation to Brexit have been more or less constant. They are also contradictory. As a result, while she is one of the least ostentatious Prime Ministers in modern history and one without much ego, she leads with political explosions erupting around her a lot of the time. She is committed to a soft border in Ireland and is also resolved to leave the customs union, a departure that makes a soft border almost impossible to secure. She considers herself to be the leader of the pro-business party, yet acts in ways that alarm many businesses.

Still she presses on. Contrary to mythology May did not contemplate resigning after the 2017 election. She is tougher than that. To save her skin, she immediately sacked her unpopular senior advisers Nick Timothy and Fiona Hill, and just carried on. By the early summer of 2018 May had stopped reading the newspapers, relying on a daily digest from media advisers. She has a small coterie of new advisers led by Gavin Barwell, a former MP.

Although lacking in guile, in the post-election manoeuvring of 2017/18 May made a Harold Wilson-like calculation that her ardent Brexit right would accept liberal Brexit terms, provided that Britain actually left the EU in March 2019. So she agreed a £39 billion Brexit deal to close the crucial initial agreement with the EU. On the same basis, she persuaded the Brexiteers to accept a 'transition' after March 2019, a delay that was laughably rechristened the 'implementation' phase even though when it was agreed nobody knew what they would be implementing. As part of her mis-timed sequence, in the summer of 2018 May sought to keep options open when she needed unyielding clarity. In seeking to leave the customs union, retain a border in Ireland and have near frictionless arrangements with the EU, May contemplated at least three options. As some despairing senior Whitehall officials have reflected, she would have been wiser to keep all options open when she was strong at the beginning of her leadership, and to narrow them resolutely as the deadline neared.

Since Margaret Thatcher, every Tory Prime Minister has fallen over Europe. May faces a much tougher task than any of them. Cameron found his renegotiation physically exhausting, moving from one capital to another in an attempt to get a robust deal. Once he secured a deal he found the task of winning over colleagues even more draining, and even more so when some key figures refused to back him. Multiply by ten thousand the scale of May's task as the clock ticks.

WORKS CITED AND FURTHER READING

CHURCHILL

Dale, Iain (ed.), *Conservative Party General Election Manifestos, 1900–1997* (London: Routledge, 1997)

Gilbert, Martin, *Winston S. Churchill, Volume VII: Road to Victory 1941–1945* (London: Heinemann, 1986)

—, *Winston S. Churchill, Volume VIII: Never Despair 1945–1965* (London: Heinemann, 1988)

—, *Churchill's Political Philosophy* (Oxford: Oxford University Press, 1981)

—, *Churchill and America* (London: Free, 2005)

Jenkins, Roy, *Churchill* (London: Pan, 2001)

Klos, Felix, *Churchill's Last Stand: The Struggle to Unite Europe* (London: I. B. Tauris, 2018)

Seldon, Anthony, *Churchill's Indian Summer: The Conservative Government 1951–55* (London: Hodder & Stoughton, 1981)

Young, Hugo, *This Blessed Plot: Britain and Europe from Churchill to Blair* (London: Macmillan, 1998)

ATTLEE

Alter, Karen J. and Steinberg, David, 'The Theory and Reality of the European Coal and Steel Community,' in Meunier, Sophie and McNamara, Kathleen R. (eds), *Making History: European Integration and Institutional Change at Fifty* (Oxford: Oxford University Press, 2007)

Attlee, Clement, *As It Happened* (London: Odhams Press, 1954)

Bew, John, *Citizen Clem*, (London: riverrun, 2016)

Cruddas, Jon, 'Attlee, the ILP and the Romantic Tradition', Attlee Memorial Lecture, University College Oxford, 28 October 2011, joncruddas.org.uk

Davis, Richard (ed.), *British Decolonisation 1918–1984*, (Newcastle: Cambridge Scholars Publishing, 2013)

Griffiths, Richard T. (ed.), *Socialist Parties and the Question of Europe in the 1950's*, (Leiden: Brill, 1993)

Harris, Kenneth, *Attlee,* (London: Orion, 1995)

Hennessy, Peter, *The Prime Minister: The Office and Its Holders Since 1945* (London: Penguin, 2001)

Ovendale, Ritchie, *The Foreign Policy of the British Labour Governments 1945–51*, (Leicester: Leicester University Press, 1984)

EDEN

Bullen, R. and Pelly, M. (eds), *Documents on British Policy Overseas*, Series II, Volume I (London: HMSO, 1986)

Eden, Anthony, *Full Circle* (London: Cassell, 1960)

Greenwood, Sean, *Britain and European Cooperation Since 1945* (Oxford: Blackwell, 1992)

Kennedy, Paul, *The Realities Behind Diplomacy* (London: Fontana, 1981)

Lamb, Richard, *The Failure of the Eden Government* (London: Sidgwick & Jackson, 1987)

Macmillan, Harold and Catterall, Peter (ed.), *The Macmillan Diaries: The Cabinet Years, 1950–1957* (London: Macmillan, 2003)

—, *The Macmillan Diaries: The Premiership 1957–1966* (London: Pan, 2012)

Dutton, David, *Anthony Eden: A Life and Reputation* (London: Arnold, 1997)

Rothwell, V., *Anthony Eden: A Political Biography 1931–1957* (Manchester: Manchester University Press, 1992)

Ruane, Kevin, *The Rise and Fall of the European Defence Community* (Basingstoke: Palgrave Macmillan, 2000)

Thorpe, D. R., *Eden: The Life and Times of Anthony Eden, First Earl of Avon, 1897–1977* (London: Chatto & Windus, 2003)

Young, J. W., 'Churchill's "No" to Europe: the "Rejection" of European Union by Churchill's Post-War Government, 1951–52', *Historical Journal* (1985), vol. 28, no. 4

MACMILLAN

Howard, Anthony, *RAB: The Life of R. A. Butler* (London: Papermac, 1987)

Macmillan, Harold, *The Memoirs of Harold Macmillan, Volumes I–IV*, (London: Macmillan, 1966)

Macmillan, Harold and Catterall, Peter (ed.), *The Macmillan Diaries: The Cabinet Years, 1950–1957* (London: Macmillan, 2003)

—, *The Macmillan Diaries: The Premiership 1957–1966* (London: Pan, 2012)

Thorpe, D. R., *Supermac: The Life of Harold Macmillan* (London: Chatto & Windus, 2010)

Williams, Charles, *Harold Macmillan* (London: Weidenfeld & Nicolson, 2009)

DOUGLAS-HOME

Dickie, John, *The Uncommon Commoner: A Study of Sir Alec Douglas-Home* (London: Pall Mall Press, 1964)

Dutton, David, *Douglas-Home* (London: Haus, 2006)

Holt, Andrew, *The Foreign Policy of the Douglas-Home Government: Britain, the United States and the End of Empire* (Basingstoke: Palgrave Macmillan, 2014)

Home, Lord, *The Way the Wind Blows: An Autobiography* (London: HarperCollins, 1976)

Hurd, Douglas, 'Home, Alexander Frederick [Alec] Douglas-, fourteenth Earl of Home and Baron Home of the Hirsel', *Oxford Dictionary of National Biography* (Oxford: Oxford University Press, 2004)

Pierre, Andrew, *Nuclear Politics: The British Experience with an Independent Strategic Force, 1939–1970* (Oxford: Oxford University Press, 1972)

Thorpe, D. R., *Alec Douglas-Home*, (London: Sinclair-Stevenson, 1997)

Young, Kenneth, *Sir Alec Douglas-Home* (London: Dent, 1970)

WILSON

Benn, Tony, *Years of Hope: Diaries, Letters and Papers 1940–62* (London: Hutchinson, 1994)

—, *Out of the Wilderness: Diaries 1963–67* (London: Hutchinson, 1987)

—, *Office Without Power: Diaries 1968–72* (London: Hutchinson, 1989)

—, *Against the Tide: Diaries 1973–76* (London: Hutchinson, 1989)

—, *Conflicts of Interest: Diaries 1977–80* (London: Hutchinson, 1990)

Coopey, Richard; Fielding, Steven and Tiratsoo, N. (eds), *The Wilson Governments, 1964–1970* (London: Pinter Publishers, 1993)

Daddow, Oliver J. (ed.), *Harold Wilson and European Integration: Britain's Second Application to Join the EEC* (London: Routledge, 2003)

Donoughue, *Bernard, Downing Street Diary: With Harold Wilson in No. 10* (London: Jonathan Cape, 2004)

—, *Prime Minister: The Conduct of Policy Under Harold Wilson & James Callaghan* (London: Jonathan Cape, 1987)

—, 'Harold Wilson: Flawed Political Genius?', Lord Speaker's Lecture 2018, www.parliament.uk

Jenkins, Roy, 'Wilson, James Harold, Baron Wilson of Rievaulx', *Oxford Dictionary of National Biography* (Oxford: Oxford University Press, 2004)

—, *A Life at the Centre* (London: Macmillan, 1991)

Parr, Helen, *Britain's Policy Towards the European Community: Harold Wilson and Britain's World Role, 1964–1967* (London: Routledge, 2005)

Pimlott, Ben, *Harold Wilson* (London: HarperCollins, 1992)

Saunders, Robert, *Yes to Europe! The 1975 Referendum and Seventies Britain* (Cambridge: Cambridge University Press, 2018)

Wall, Stephen, *The Official History of Britain and the European Community, Volume II: From Rejection to Referendum, 1963–1975* (London: Routledge, 2012)

Wilson, Harold, *A Personal Record: The Labour Government 1964–1970* (London: Weidenfeld & Nicolson, 1971)

—, *Final Term: The Labour Government 1974–1976* (London: Weidenfeld & Nicolson, 1979)

HEATH

Heath, Edward, *Travels* (London: Sidgwick & Jackson, 1977)

—, *The Course of My Life* (London: Hodder & Stoughton, 1998)

Hurd, Douglas, 'Heath, Sir Edward Richard George', in *Oxford Dictionary of National Biography* (Oxford: Oxford University Press, 2004)

—, *Memoirs* (London: Little, Brown, 2003)

McManus, Michael, *Edward Heath: A Singular Life* (London: Elliott & Thompson, 2016)

Patterson, Ben, *The Conservative Party and Europe* (London: John Harper Publishing, 2011)

Ziegler, Philip, *Edward Heath* (London: HarperPress, 2010)

CALLAGHAN

Callaghan, James, *Time & Chance* (London: HarperCollins 1987)

Donoughue, Bernard, *Downing Street Diary: Volume 2: With James Callaghan in No. 10* (London: Pimlico, 2009)

Gowland, David, *Britain and the European Union* (London: Routledge, 2016)

Healey, Denis, *The Time Of My Life* (London: Michael Joseph, 1989)

Morgan, Kenneth, *Callaghan: A Life* (Oxford: Oxford University Press, 1997)

Owen, David, *Time To Declare: Second Innings* (London: Politco's, 1991)

Saunders, Robert, *Yes to Europe! The 1975 Referendum and Seventies Britain* (Cambridge: Cambridge University Press, 2018)

THATCHER

Cockfield, Arthur, *The European Union: Creating the Single Market* (London: Wiley, 1994)

Hurd, Douglas, *Memoirs* (London: Little, Brown, 2003)

Lawson, Nigel, *The View From No. 11* (London: Corgi, 1993)

Major, John, *John Major: The Autobiography* (London: HarperCollins, 1999)

Moore, Charles, *Margaret Thatcher: The Authorized Biography – Volume One: Not For Turning* (London: Allen Lane, 2013)

—, *Margaret Thatcher: The Authorized Biography – Volume Two: Everything She Wants* (London: Allen Lane, 2016)

Thatcher, Margaret, *The Downing Street Years* (London: HarperCollins, 1993)
—, 'The Bruges Speech', www.margaretthatcher.org

MAJOR

Major, John, *John Major: The Autobiography* (London: HarperCollins, 1999)
Patten, Chris, *First Confession: A Sort of Memoir* (London: Allen Lane, 2017)
Seldon, Anthony, *Major: A Political Life* (London: Weidenfeld & Nicolson, 1997)

BLAIR

Blair, Tony, *A Journey* (London: Hutchinson, 2010)
Campbell, Alastair, *The Alastair Campbell Diaries, Volume One: Prelude to Power 1994–1997* (London: Arrow, 2010)
—, *The Alastair Campbell Diaries, Volume Two: Power and the People 1997–1999* (London: Hutchinson, 2011)
—, *The Alastair Campbell Diaries, Volume Three: Power and Responsibility 1999–2001* (London: Hutchinson, 2011)
—, *The Alastair Campbell Diaries, Volume Four: The Burden of Power – Countdown to Iraq 2001–2003* (London: Hutchinson, 2012),
—, *The Alastair Campbell Diaries, Volume Five: Outside, Inside, 2003–2005* (London: Biteback Publishing, 2016)
—, *The Alastair Campbell Diaries, Volume Six: From Blair to Brown, 2005–2007* (London: Biteback Publishing, 2017)

Liddle, Roger, *The Europe Dilemma: Britain and the Challenges of EU Integration* (London: I. B. Tauris, 2014)

Mandelson, Peter, *The Third Man: Life at the Heart of New Labour* (London: HarperPress, 2010)

Wall, Stephen, *A Stranger in Europe: Britain and the EU from Thatcher to Blair* (Oxford: Oxford University Press, 2008)

BROWN

Brown, Gordon, *Britain: Leading, Not Leaving – The Patriotic Case for Remaining in Europe* (Selkirk: Deerpark Press, 2016)

—, *My Life, Our Times* (London: Bodley Head, 2017)

Rawnsley, Andrew, *The End of the Party: The Rise and Fall of New Labour* (London: Viking, 2010)

Richards, Steve, *Whatever It Takes: The Inside Story of Gordon Brown and New Labour* (London: Fourth Estate, 2009)

CAMERON

Goodwin, Matthew and Ford, Robert, *Revolt on the Right: Explaining Support for the Radical Right in Britain* (London: Routledge, 2013)

Letwin, Oliver, *Hearts and Minds: The Battle for the Conservative Party from Thatcher to the Present* (London: Biteback Publishing, 2017)

Oakeshott, Isabel and Ashcroft, Michael, *Call Me Dave* (London: Biteback Publishing, 2015)

Seldon, Anthony and Snowdon, Peter, *Cameron at 10: The Inside Story 2010–15* (London: William Collins, 2015)

Shipman, Tim, *All Out War: The Full Story of How Brexit sank Britain's Political Class* (London: William Collins, 2016)

MAY

Hutton, Will and Adonis, Andrew, *Saving Britain: How We Must Change to Prosper in Europe* (London: Abacus, 2018)

Shipman, Tim, *Fall Out: A Year of Political Mayhem* (London: William Collins, 2017)